CW00495243

DETAIL IN CONTEMPORARY RETAIL DESIGN

Published in 2012 by
Laurence King Publishing Ltd
361–373 City Road
London
EC1V 1LR
e-mail: enquiries@laurenceking.com
www.laurenceking.com

A catalogue record for this book is
available from the British Library

ISBN: 978 1 85669 741 5

Designed by Olga Reid
Cover design by Hamish Muir
Project Editor: Gaynor Sermon

Printed in China

DETAIL IN CONTEMPORARY RETAIL DESIGN

**DREW PLUNKETT
AND OLGA REID**

LAURENCE KING PUBLISHING

CONTENTS

INTRODUCTION

Good retail interiors should inspire, persuade and reassure. They should fine tune the familiar and deliver the unexpected, confounding presumptions and exceeding expectations. They need designers who understand the references and can make the gestures that will reverberate most clearly in shoppers' conscious and unconscious imaginations, but – to make such conceptual strategies and tactics effective – those designers need to understand not just the cultural resonance of form and materials but also their technical performance, not only the mechanics of construction but also the aesthetic refinement of detail.

Clients, whether independent or corporate, now willingly accept that the creation of appropriate retailing environments is an essential component in their business plans, and their commitment owes everything to the objective evidence, consistently demonstrated in sales returns, of the positive impact of the right interior on sales.

Shopping is a tribal activity, defined by brand loyalties, which are as likely to be directed towards a supermarket chain as they are to the most esoteric of small independent shops. Design's role is to define brand identity and then to re-define it because few solutions have an effective life span of more than five years. Retail interiors need to change, in order to demonstrate that the business they represent is moving on and improving. Re-design has to judge and make the changes that will attract new shoppers to the tribe without alienating the old. The inevitable disappearance of the best interiors may be regrettable but that is an acknowledgement that every good interior has something that encapsulates, in its particular formulation of materials and techniques, the time of its creation.

Design solutions are driven by perceptions of the needs and preferences of targeted customers who have come to expect that the things they buy, other than the most utilitarian essentials, will be complemented by the interiors in which they buy them. Increasingly, customers share with designers an understanding of the interaction between social and design conventions and can interpret the languages and dialects of commercial interior design – which they have assimilated – while shopping.

The exterior of a shop and the building that contains it are registered briefly, if noticed at all, and the niceties of their construction are of little significance to those who pass inside. Once inside, however, customers are unavoidably in intimate proximity to the materials and the construction details that have redefined the walls, floor, ceiling and the objects contained within them. Qualities of detailing may only register subliminally but, while customers focus on merchandise, the small-scale details of the building fabric are present in their peripheral vision to underpin, or undermine, their perception of a product's worth.

Retail details usually need to be a little discreet, supportive of the merchandise, offering shoppers quiet confirmation that they have found the right place in which to conduct their search. In the simple shells of shop units on streets and in malls, with their rectilinear plans and modest ceiling heights, there is little room for grandiloquence. Occasionally an attention seeking gesture is called for but, no matter how dramatic it may be, it will fail if the details of its construction are handled clumsily. Whether grand gesture or no gesture, it is the considered sum of finely detailed parts that strikes the convincing collective note.

Prices and rents, taxes and services in good retailing locations mean that, once a client has possession of the shell, there is an imperative that construction and installation should finish quickly so that income generation can begin quickly. This pressure encourages prefabrication off site and collaboration between designer and maker to find the most efficient means of production. The exterior envelope deals with weathering and security and encourages speculation about a range of untried and untested materials within it, but no designer can expect to have the body of practical knowledge needed to implement effectively the complete palette of options. Conversations with specialist manufacturers and fabricators at the earliest stages of project development will introduce information about performance and implementation that will shape intelligent detailing. There is never virtue in contrived forms and complicated construction. There is always economic virtue in finding the simplest way of making and, when something is easier to make, it is likely to be better made. The specialist maker is best equipped to find that way.

The designer's role is to initiate, to define the aesthetic and to recognize unseen and untested potential that those who are necessarily involved with practicalities cannot see. Designers orchestrate project development, frequently producing drawings that do no more than define form, set out dimensions and specify materials, providing crucial basic information for the specialists who are increasingly taking responsibility for producing detailed drawings, for their own information and the designer's approval.

Local economies have an impact. In some the availability of cheap but comparatively unskilled labour determines construction methods and therefore the nature of detailing, in which manual imprecision prevails over machined precision and a virtue must be made of it. There are others where surviving artisanal skills extend options and feed the designer's imagination with unfamiliar possibilities. Artisans survive, still capable of stamping an interior with the unique marks of their crafts and skills, but their contribution is increasingly challenged by technology, by the digital interaction of computer aided design and computer aided manufacture, which makes the production of intricate, perfectly wrought components more affordable and better suited to the increasingly global nature of interior design practice. Details generated in one hemisphere may now be produced locally in the other and the degree of precision and standard of production will be assured.

Retailing is a global activity, but there is not necessarily a global solution. Buildings and the streets and malls that contain them give context to empty retail shells and there are contexts where the flamboyant gesture is essential and others where it is absurd. The new cities that are mushrooming in the developing world require designers to pump life and identity into the proliferation of anonymous interior spaces. Older cities offer idiosyncrasies and less anonymous empty shells that may require, and deserve, less drama.

The traditional configuration of the shop window, with merchandise displayed against a screen that obscures views of the interior, has disappeared. With few exceptions shops now operate behind a fully glazed façade that presents views of the interior and its set pieces to the street. It is as important for interiors to signal 'cheap' as it is to signal 'expensive', to filter out the customers who do not want to use them, and those who cannot afford to use them.

Shops that sell cheap goods rely on fast turnover to compensate for small profit margins, and signal their strategy with modest finishes and utilitarian displays. They offer few aesthetic refinements and rely on strategic planning to move customers efficiently around the merchandise, occasionally exposing them to the temptations of impulse buying. They favour self-service operation, dense product display and checkout desks or, increasingly, self-service checkouts that further reduce the expensive component of staff costs in equations with low profit margins.

Typically, such operations supply necessities and have had little need for the seductive interior. Detailing is expedient and fittings are generic, but, as customers become increasingly acclimatized to levels of refinement in the other interiors they use, expectations rise and must be met. Brands match their immediate rivals on prices and mimic each other's successful products. Increasingly, all they have left with which to compete is the quality of the interior experience they offer, no matter how financially constrained it may be. When quality and price become indistinguishable the interior must imply some degree of distinction. At the very cheapest end of the market it must signal cheapest and does so by expedient default.

Interiors selling luxury goods massage perceptions of quality and filter out inappropriate customers by declaring their exclusivity, which they demonstrate by extravagant use of floor space and sparse product displays. Staff are discreetly attentive and final sales transactions are tactful. Planning strategy remains crucial but quality and exclusivity are most clearly expressed in the selection and detailed assembly of finishes and fittings.

Between the extremes of necessity and luxury are those mainstream shops that look for a profitable balance of turnover and competitive prices. Their target customers have varying degrees of modest disposable income but share an ambition to move away from the entry-level experience. For those who design such environments there is the conundrum of weighing the cost of construction against potential profit, density of display against clarity. It is in these projects, typically chain stores, that collaboration between client team and design team is most likely to be close as customer profiles are debated and defined and detailing strategies are evolved; and it is these interiors that have the shortest life span, as they are consistently restyled to reaffirm their presence and competitive edge.

A good retail designer has to be objective, not excessively concerned with winning peer approval, happy to identify, adopt and adapt the aesthetic preferences of target customers but always obliged to innovate, to present something that, while unfamiliar, excites as it communicates the recognized, or redefined, brand values to an extended family of old and new customers. That solution cannot be contrived by market research, which may support the uninspired but offers less to creative retail designers who have an instinct that allows them to sense, anticipate and give definition to shifts in public taste. Formulaic research has been compared to looking in a mirror, which reveals what lies behind but hides what lies ahead. That is best found in the designer's intuition and imagination and given definitive form in creative expression of detail.

This collection of recently completed projects recognizes and demonstrates that, regardless of budget, the good interior depends on creative detail. It includes interiors that are complex in construction and those that achieve their impact with the simplest of means. It documents innovative uses of materials and technologies and the detailing that supports them. The introductory text to each project describes their context and broad intention, and photographs and drawings explain detailed strategies and tactics. It is unlikely that the ideas illustrated can be directly transplanted into other shells in other places because every interior should be particular to its context and often the greater its particularity the greater its impact, but the principles they embody may be freshly interpreted, to continue the evolution of the detailing languages of retail design.

ACCESSORIES

AKTIPIS,
PATRAS
POINT SUPREME ARCHITECTS

The shell of the original flower shop was stripped of all existing display elements and work surfaces. These were replaced by 14 free-standing tables that were grouped in the middle of the floor area and are, between them, capable of meeting all the practical demands of preparing, displaying and selling flowers and plants.

The tables have square wooden legs of varying lengths, and the basic module, defined by the tile with which they are clad, determines the dimensions of their tops. The diversity of table types allows the layout to be reorganized in response to seasonal variation in the flowers available. The heights are organized so that tables may pass over and under others. The sheen of the white tiled tables and the white painted floor combine to make a complementary background for the colours of flowers and plants.

The walls are covered with bespoke paper printed with enlarged images, sourced from an old print of jungle vegetation, which creates abstracted organic shapes. Images of birds, taken from an old encyclopaedia, interact with the mundane modern technical details, making a virtue of electrical sockets and drainage outlets by allowing them to contribute to the joke. The sound of birdsong, the plastic lizards left on tabletops and garden chairs contribute to the light-hearted allusion to exterior space.

The new façade incorporates a recycled steel door, with a complex filigree pattern that suggests vegetation and is painted white to match floor and tables. Areas of the window glass are embossed with leaf patterns and the window is set back as far as possible to make space for a display table on the street.

RIGHT
Plan
1 Open air display
2 Central table grouping
3 Counter
4 Stairs to mezzanine

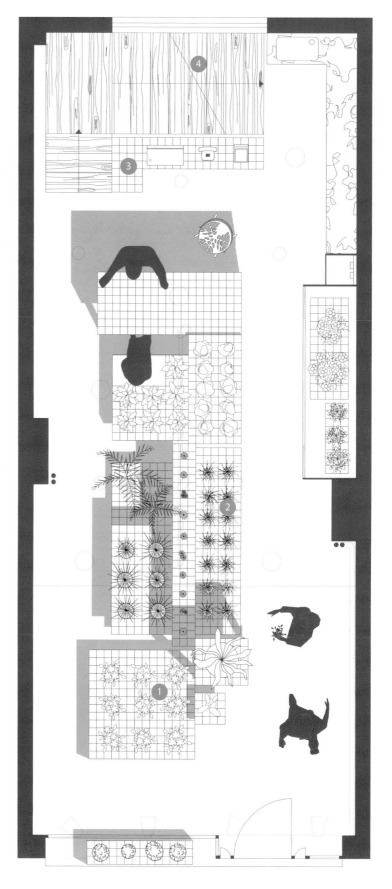

PLAN, SCALE 1:50

ELEVATION, SCALE 1:100

ABOVE
Tile-topped tables at various heights occupy the middle of the floor. The façade is set back to make space for open air display.

LEFT
Elevation
1 Open air display
2 Central table grouping
3 Counter
4 Stairs to mezzanine
5 Mezzanine

LEFT
The walls are lined with bespoke paper printed with enlarged, slightly abstracted images of vegetation.

BELOW
Images of birds interact with practical service elements such as this electrical plug socket.

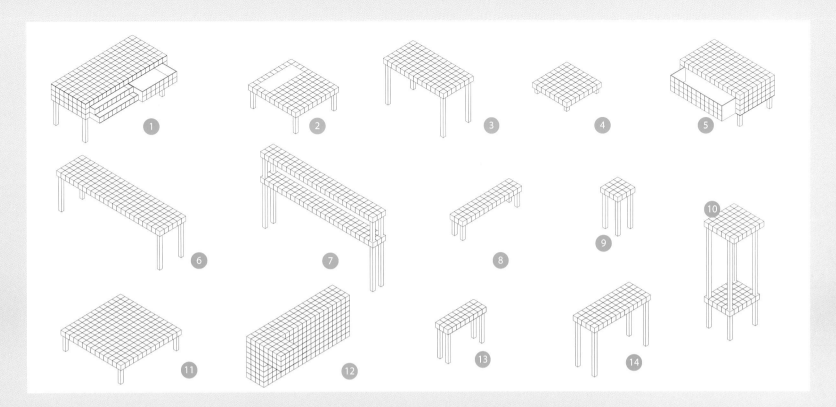

ABOVE

Table types
1 Cashier/preparation table
2 Low table/client seat
3 High table for low plants
4 Low table for big, heavy plants
5 Table with pot storage drawer

6 High and long table for medium-sized plants
7 High, narrow, long table for small pots and plants
8 Table for external space pots
9 Table for special plants

10 Table for plants with hanging fronds
11 Exhibition table for external space pots
12 Table for computer, fax and phone
13 Table in refrigerator
14 Small table for refrigerator

BELOW RIGHT

Tables carry and frame cut flowers and pot plants

BELOW LEFT

Plan of table layout

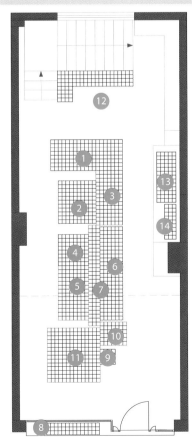

PLAN, SCALE 1:100

BOODLES, LONDON
EVA JIRICNA ARCHITECTS

The designers of this project have evolved a well-researched and tested visual language in which glass and steel, their signature materials, are pushed to the limits of structural capabilities. Their distinctive vocabulary offers a formula that is well suited to making the interior of a jewellery shop, and their clients, for whom they have carried out a number of commissions, here gave enthusiastic support for a radical reinterpretation of the traditional, conservative values of the jewellery trade.

The view to the new interior, from one of London's most busy and fashionable shopping streets, is partially filtered by a serpentine row of floor-to-ceiling glass tubes, each with a dichroic insert that changes colour with changing angles of vision and lighting. Behind this a curved, backlit reception desk doubles as a bar to welcome customers. A mirror-clad wall around an existing staircase partially shields the sales area.

A translucent glass wall, supported on an engineered mild steel structure, lines the wall behind the reception/bar and contains within it backlighting for the triangular glass cabinets. In front of these a stone-tiled strip leads to the semicircular steel and glass stair that occupies the full width of the shop. The rest of the floor is carpeted and on it sit glass-topped sales tables under a refurbished, translucent rooflight, which also brings natural light, down the generous void with its translucent stair, to the basement.

The delicate, ostensibly fragile, stair is the dominant element in the interior. Its broad sweep is defined by the central steel stringer that supports its glass treads. These are stabilized by struts that tie their outer edges back to the stringer and provide fixings for the curved glass balustrade. The mirror-clad wall behind, stretching through two floors, duplicates the intricate tracery of the stair and the rooflight that hangs above it.

TOP RIGHT
Stone floor tiles, in front of the triangular backlit glass cabinets, lead to the stair. Carpet defines the consultation and sales area. The rooflight provides natural light. The whole is reflected in the mirrors on the back wall of the stairwell.

BOTTOM RIGHT
The glass treads seen through the glass balustrade appear to dematerialize and highlight the stair's apparent fragility.

OPPOSITE PAGE
Dichroic inserts provide changing colour within the floor-to-ceiling glass tubes that partially block views of the interior from the street. The backlit desk offers customer hospitality.

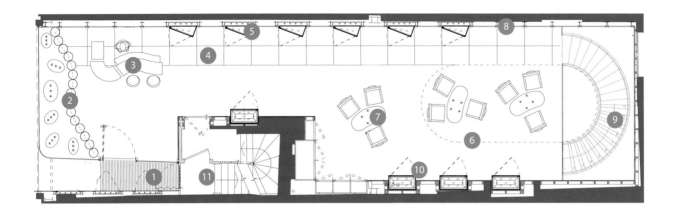

GROUND FLOOR PLAN, SCALE 1:100

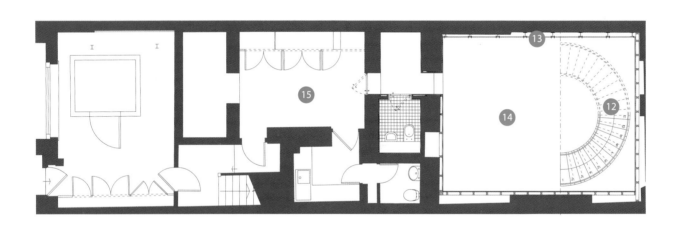

BASEMENT PLAN, SCALE 1:100

ABOVE TOP
1 Entrance
2 Glass tubes with dichroic inserts
3 Counter
4 Stone floor tiles
5 Display cabinets on translucent glass wall
6 Line of rooflight above
7 Consultation table
8 Mirror-clad wall to stairwell
9 Stairwell
10 Display cabinets
11 Stair to upper floors

ABOVE BOTTOM
12 Stair
13 Mirror-clad wall
14 Lower consultation area
15 Services and storage

OPPOSITE PAGE, TOP
1 Glass tubes with dichroic inserts
2 Triangular display cabinets on translucent glass wall
3 Mirror-clad wall to stairwell
4 Stair
5 Rooflight

OPPOSITE PAGE, BOTTOM
At basement level the central steel string, wider at its base to spread its load and sitting above the floor on five feet, rears up and away from its reflection.

SECTION, SCALE 1:100

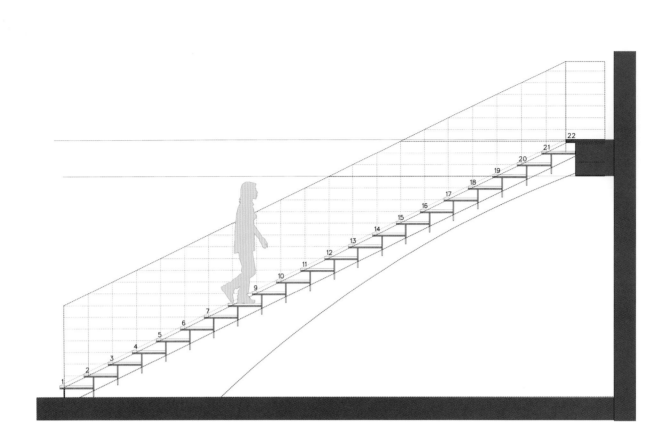

UNFOLDED ELEVATION, SCALE 1:50

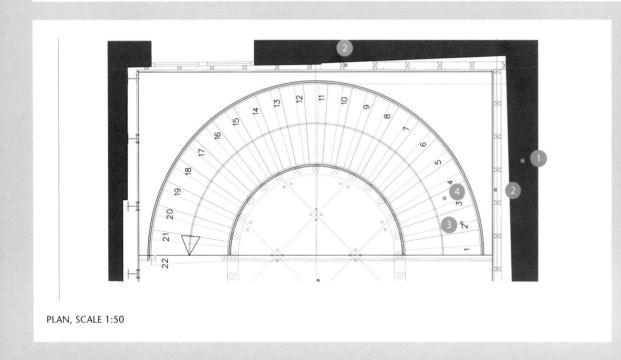

PLAN, SCALE 1:50

TOP
The unwound elevation of the outside curve.

LEFT
Geometric irregularities are eliminated by relining existing walls in response to the perfect semicircle of the stair.

Plan of stair
1 Existing walls
2 Mirror on plywood or timber stud framing
3 Glass riser
4 Glass tread

RIGHT
The stair, the lower consulting room and entrance to the secure area behind are reflected in the two-storey-high mirrors.

BELOW
1 Glass balustrade
2 Steel stringer
3 Glass riser
4 Glass tread

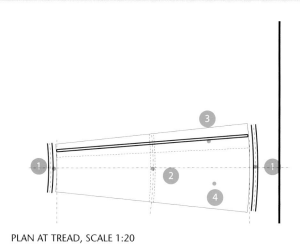

PLAN AT TREAD, SCALE 1:20

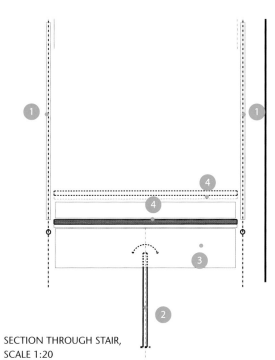

SECTION THROUGH STAIR,
SCALE 1:20

DRESSLER PAPETERIE, MUNICH
EINS:33

This family-run business is located in the main shopping arcade of Grünwald, an expensive and fashionable suburb of Munich. It offers high-quality paper products and desk accessories. The surface of the timber boards has affinities with the surface of specialist papers, while the clarity with which the boards are assembled has the simplicity and precision of carefully folded paper. The perfection of the finished assembly demonstrates the advantages of recognizing and respecting a material's natural capacities.

Wooden boards, 300mm (11¾in.) wide and of varying lengths, with 1mm (½sin.)-wide joints, are used throughout for floors, new areas of wall and furniture units. Horizontal and vertical joints line through precisely to suggest that boards are ribbons that run across floors and over furniture without interruption. When boards are reorientated through 90 degrees, the weaving of verticals and horizontals defines areas within the plan.

The ceiling and existing walls are painted plaster. New wall and floorboards stop short of or sit in front of them to maintain visual integrity, and the separation is accentuated by concealed light sources and the shadows they cast.

Three different counter and display units conform to the geometry set up by the floorboards. White laminated MDF drawers allow clear expression of the two dimensionality of the timber boards that form tabletops. The front edges of shelves butt against the back face of the boards that support them, and both elements are connected but intact.

Scrupulous and ingenious small-scale detailing eliminates the visual clutter that would interfere with the purity of the whole. A ribbon dispenser is concealed behind a wall board, with only the ribbon ends exposed. Slots are precisely milled into a shelf to hold the bottom edge of greeting cards. The owners' dachshund is kennelled behind the counter.

RIGHT
Boards on the floor, walls and furniture line through precisely and determine the geometry and dimensions of plan and elevations.

PLAN, SCALE 1:50

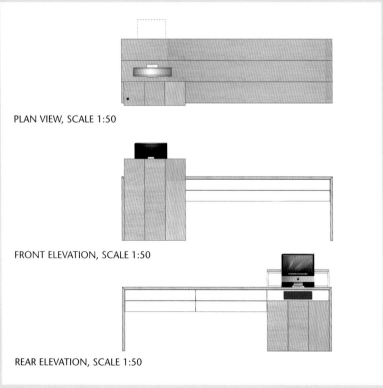

PLAN VIEW, SCALE 1:50

FRONT ELEVATION, SCALE 1:50

REAR ELEVATION, SCALE 1:50

ABOVE
Floor plan
1 Entrance
2 Display tables
3 Counter
4 Widened shelf in window recess
5 Kitchen
6 Storage areas

LEFT
Counter plan view, front and
rear elevations
The counter is three boards
(900mm/35⅜in.) wide, as is the front
vertical element, which masks the
computer and the dachshund's bed.

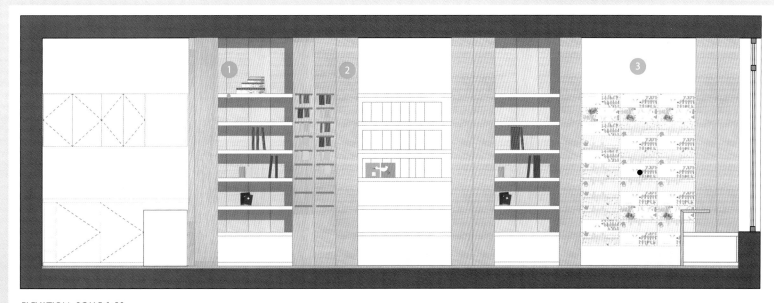

ELEVATION, SCALE 1:50

ABOVE
Shelving is contained within the 300mm (11¾in.)-wide zone between vertical boards and the existing plastered walls.
1 Shelves
2 Vertical boards
3 Plastered walls

RIGHT
Right-angle joints are mitred to suggest a continuous end grain. The white melamine drawer fronts sustain the impression of the timber board as a ribbon running continuously over horizontal and vertical surfaces.

LABOSHOP, PARIS
MATHIEU LEHANNEUR

LaboShop is the public face of LaboBrain and together they constitute Laboratoire, which is described as an 'innovation catalyst where pioneering artists and scientists collaborate to create new forms of art and design with cultural, economic, humanitarian and educational ramifications.'

While LaboBrain houses the 'think tank', LaboShop is described as a 'design and innovation store' where prototypes produced by the Laboratoire organization may be seen, tested and bought. At night it also houses FoodLab, 'a place for culinary and molecular experimentation', and the retail display elements that occupy the centre of the floor during the day retract to ceiling level to become light sources.

The rise and fall of the vitrines, which are rationally cubic, declares the organization's commitment to the fusion of science and art. The electrically powered folding arm mechanism is transparently simple and, when fully retracted, is concealed within a plaster downstand whose curves allow it to blend seamlessly into the ceiling plane. The success of the whole depends on this refined detailing and the high standard of making and installation. The precise matching of colour tones and reflectivity in walls, ceiling and display installation confirm that this is an aesthetic shaped by scientific objectivity rather than subjective gesture. Less formal, expedient intrusions, such as the black power cables that hang from the perimeter lighting recess, underline the perfection of the major elements.

When objective decision making is thus carried to its conclusion, its clear logic offers visitors the key to recognizing and analyzing the decision-making process and a first gentle workout in the 'mental gymnasium' that Laboratoire declares itself to be.

TOP RIGHT
The perimeter recess provides lighting over the seating and a power source. The curved section of the cantilevered shelves responds to the curves of the downstand that houses the vitrines.

RIGHT
The 'rise and fall' mechanism is self-evidently simple, an expression of a rational aesthetic.

OPPOSITE PAGE
Cuboid vitrines emerge from and retreat into the ceiling downstand, which is visually eased into the ceiling plane by radiused junctions.

LOTTE, SEOUL
UNIVERSAL DESIGN STUDIO

Concession outlets – specialist shops operating independently within a larger department store – have to establish their identity in relationship both to the store itself and rival concessions within it. Avenuel, five floors of specialist shops under a cinema and spa, is the luxury shopping flagship for the Lotte department store. The two units shown here, located on open sided 'islands' between circulation routes and other branded concessions, are distinguished from more conventional, lighter, brighter neighbours by a palette of dark, reflective materials.

The first area, on the second floor, houses men's accessories at one end and a jewellery boutique at the other, the two separated by a circulation passage. The accessories unit is defined by a 10m (33ft) long luggage display plinth intended to suggest an airport luggage carousel around which are grouped free-standing low level cabinets with glass sides and tops, to show smaller products. The territory of the jewellery boutique next to the passage is marked by a line of faceted display columns, clad in mirror panels above and below the eye level display cabinets with angled glass screens on the other three sides.

The third floor concession, for shoes and leather goods, is defined by a formalized landscape of triangular backlit tables under a triangular grid of black acrylic ceiling panels. The fumigated oak flooring contributes to the dark background. The idea of landscape is consolidated by a triangular pool of water on the surface of which float flower petals. The tall display units adopt a more conventional rectangular geometry. Corian shelves are supported on painted metal frames, which are in turn supported on structural glass fins. Integrated lighting illuminates products above and below.

ABOVE
Leather goods – third floor : A 'landscape' of triangular ceiling panels and tabletops and a petal-strewn pool.

RIGHT
Second floor plan: men's accessories to the left, jewellery to the right.
1 Shoe display
2 Shoe display and seating
3 Small luxury goods table
4 Shoe storage
5 Luggage display
6 Vertical display cases
7 Jewellery display
8 Jewellery display counter
9 Faceted glass screen
10 Personal service counter
11 Passage

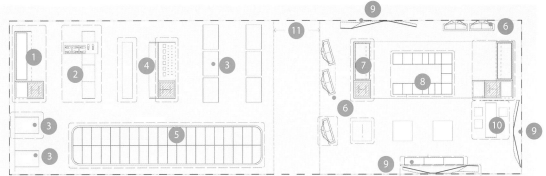

SECOND FLOOR
PLAN, SCALE 1:200

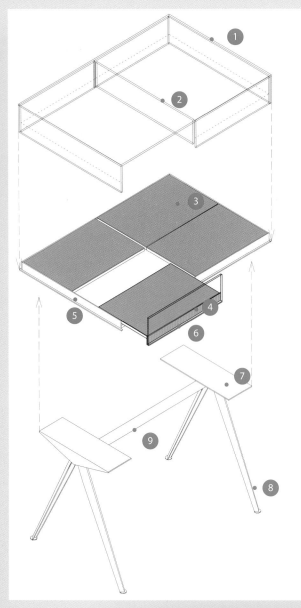

ABOVE & LEFT
Small luxury goods table
1 Clear UV bonded glass canopy, 12mm (½in.) for fixed panes, 10mm (⅜in.) for drawer panes
2 12mm (½in.) central glass support rib clamped to base
3 Leather bonded to plywood drawer base, edged with brushed stainless steel angles
4 Glass area bonded to stainless steel angles, with proprietary glass adhesive tape, back painted with mirror silvering
5 Stainless steel angle fixed to drawer on long sides
6 Stainless steel angle fixed to short sides
7 6mm (¼in.) powder-coated welded and folded steel plates fixed to underside of drawer
8 6mm (¼in.) powder coated steel angled legs with 60mm (2½in.)-diameter feet with rubber pad
9 60mm (2½in.)-diameter powder-coated steel tube welded to legs and folded plates

BELOW
Men's accessories, second floor: display tables contain small products.

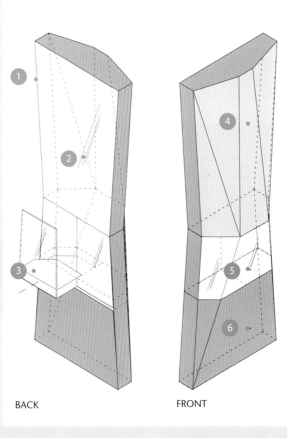

BACK   FRONT

FAR LEFT
Jewellery area – second floor: display
'columns' are clad in faceted mirror
above and below glass display cabinets.

LEFT
1 Anti-reflective glass panel back painted
at edges to conceal steel frame
2 Back-painted faceted glass interior
3 Double extension display drawers with
anti-reflective glass fronts
4 Faceted blue glass panels
5 Anti-reflective clear glass panels
6 Back-painted faceted glass base

BELOW
7 Anti-reflective glass panel displaying
back-painted interior faceted panels
(shown dotted) bonded to concealed
steel frame
8 Glass area back painted to conceal steel
frame
9 Double extension display drawers with
ant-reflective glass fronts
10 Concealed opening for access to
integrated services
11 Faceted glass base back painted to
conceal structure, drawer runners and
lighting
12 Protective edge to base
13 Faceted blue anti-reflective glass
panels fixed to powder-coated steel
structure
14 Faceted clear anti-reflective glass
panels fixed to powder-coated steel
structure
15 Head structure of case extended above
finished ceiling line and mechanically
fixed to rigid element
16 Powder-coated steel frame bonded to
faceted glass panels
17 Anti-reflective glass panel bonded to
concealed steel structure
18 Concealed LED lighting
19 Concealed double extension drawer
runners to provide access to display
surface
20 Case base sunk below finished floor
level with protective edge

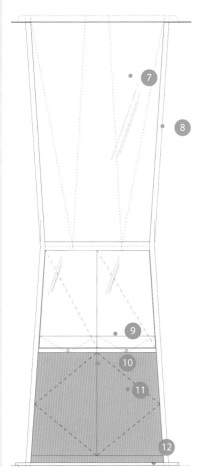

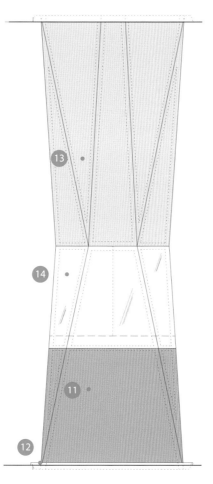

DETAIL, SCALE 1:25

LEFT
The colours, illumination and reflectivity of the shelves match the triangular elements in the centre of the island.

BELOW
Glass shelving unit
1 Shelf trays with concealed lighting supported on glass fins with custom-made copper fixings
2 Powder-coated paint on metal shelf tray sides
3 Laminated glass fins supported by prefabricated foot and clamped above finished ceiling level
4 Black cloth-covered electrical cable from above ceiling level
5 Polished copperplated prefabricated foot

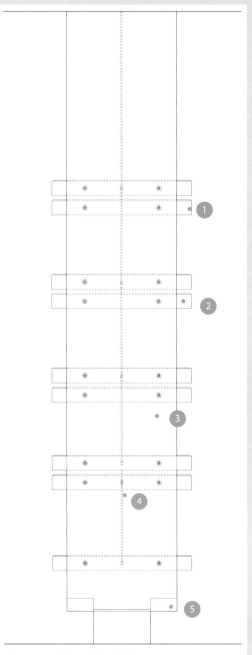

SIDE ELEVATION, SCALE 1:10

RIGHT

Leather goods – third floor: the glass supporting panels have a minimal presence and give the shelving system a rigidity impossible to achieve with suspension wires.

BELOW

Exploded axonometric of shelf units

1 Clear laminated glass fin supported by fabricated foot and clamped head above finished ceiling level

2 6mm (¼in.) Corian glued to 12mm (½in.) plywood

3 Shelf sides formed from bent metal flat

4 Single welded joint polished smooth

5 Steel bracket welded to metal sides below plywood to support copper fixings

6 Powder-coated paint finish

7 Shelves supported on 4 custom-made copper fixings passing through glass and shelf sides into bracket

8 Concealed fluorescent strip light

9 Black cloth-covered lighting cable from ceiling

10 Hollow copper tube with disc stopper located between glass and shelf

11 Copper allen key fastener passing through glass and sleeve

12 Powder-coated steel upstand with holes to receive copper fixing supports

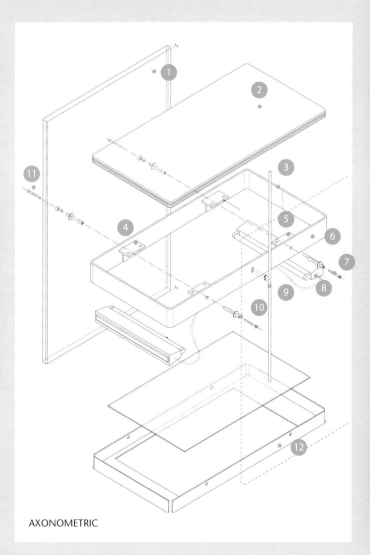

AXONOMETRIC

OPTICON, HAMBURG
GRAFT

Opticians' shops are obliged to present customers with an abundance of choices because the cosmetic value of glasses is at least as important as the optical qualities. All must be easily accessible for browsing and selection.

The side walls of this long, deep site are wholly devoted to shelving on which pairs of glasses sit loosely for easy removal, examination and replacement by customers. The fluid curves of the shelves disguise both casual replacement and irregularities in the existing perimeter walls. Seemingly random highlights along the lengths of the shelves, illuminated with brand identification plaques, create a second, more staccato rhythm. The flexibility offered by the long, unbroken lengths of shelving copes comfortably with inconsistencies in the lengths of sections devoted to individual brands.

The centre of the narrow plan is occupied by the continuous slab that acts as a counter and informal consultation area. This slab, which appears to be extravagantly cantilevered, is supported along its length by existing columns that are reshaped and clad in mirror to disguise them. The form of the counter is a development of the theme first expressed at the entrance by a bulbous abstracted form, nominally a seat, that interacts with the change in level. Red velvet upholstery defines and connects the two.

The red is anticipated by a fragment of carpet at the entrance, which quickly gives way to white that covers the rest of the floor, deadening sound as customers move away from the street and are drawn deeper into concentrated selection. The red and white sections are connected at the stairs by a tracery of red tendrils woven into the white ground.

TOP
Shelving establishes the horizontal emphasis that draws the eye into and around the interior.

RIGHT
Seating interlocks with the change of level at the entrance, establishing the form and materials that evolve into the counter beyond.

OPPOSITE PAGE
The red pattern in the carpet links the entrance space to the counter, which dominates the upper display and selection zones. Two of the three re-clad and mirrored columns provide discreet support for the cantilever.

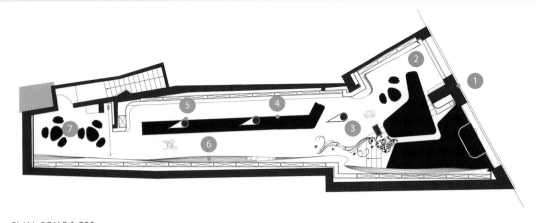

PLAN, SCALE 1:200

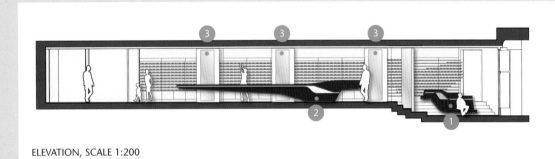

ELEVATION, SCALE 1:200

LEFT
Plan
1 Entrance
2 Built-in seating
3 Carpet pattern
4 Counter
5 Reshaped mirror-clad columns
6 Perimeter shelving
7 Loose seating

MIDDLE
Elevation
1 Built-in seating
2 Counter
3 Re-shaped mirror-clad columns

BELOW
Brand name inserts are placed where appropriate along the neutral length of shelves.

RIGHT
Illuminated acrylic plaques sit loosely on and punctuate the lengths of shelving.

BELOW
The predominant front edge of the shelf accepts the informal return of spectacles by browsing customers.

ORMONDE JAYNE, LONDON
CAULDER MOORE

The shops in London's scrupulously preserved arcades are, almost without exception, devoted to the sale of luxury goods. Behind their individual façades, which invariably conform to a common decorative scheme, their floor areas are small and their ceilings disproportionately high. A tight stair usually leads to a mezzanine storage level. Most necessarily carry limited stock and display it with restrained panache.

This perfumery rejects the option of a reproduction interior sympathetic to the façade. The dark-coloured walls and ceiling minimize the impact of existing mouldings and the traditional values they imply. The new display structure of apparently randomly stacked glossy black boxes, resting on an incongruously light timber floor, sets up an alternative design language that is more cubist than classical. The brand's orange product boxes provide counterpoints of colour. Bottles are principally displayed on glass shelves against a mirrored wall to complement their transparency and reflectivity.

Some of the stacked boxes at lower levels contain storage drawers, and the mitred edges of the drawer fronts camouflage their presence so that evidence of a necessary but mundane storage provision is minimized. Drawers are pulled open by a groove cut in the underside of each front panel to provide a finger grip. A self-closing mechanism pulls and holds the drawer shut. All drawer and static structure boxes are finished with a 1mm (½sin.) pencil-rounded edge to prevent chipping of MDF arrises or paint finish. Other utilitarian elements – the till, computer and radiator – are concealed within the box units that make up the cash and wrap desk.

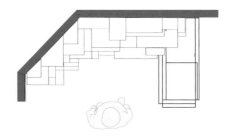

PLAN, SCALE 1:50

TOP
The façade complies with the arcade's shared decorative scheme.

MIDDLE
Plan
The till, computer and radiator are contained within the unit shown red.

BOTTOM
Elevation
Drawer units are shown in red.

OPPOSITE PAGE, TOP LEFT
The cash and wrap desk conceals the radiator, till and computer within appropriately sized 'boxes'. The brand's orange packaging provides a counterpoint to the black gloss of the display 'boxes'. The stair leads to the mezzanine storage.

OPPOSITE PAGE, TOP RIGHT
Dark painted existing walls, ceiling

and mouldings recede and the glossy black stacked 'boxes' become the dominant motif.

OPPOSITE PAGE, BOTTOM LEFT
Axonometric shows red display 'boxes' that operate as storage drawers.

OPPOSITE PAGE, BOTTOM RIGHT
Detail of storage drawers
1 External and interior surfaces receive the same gloss paint finish
2 Mitred edges
3 Both drawer and frame have mitred edges
4 20mm (¾in.)-deep and 15mm (⅝in.)-high groove cut into base of drawer front to provide grip for opening
5 Internal face of mitre and drawer painted to match exterior faces
6 Black sprayed stop cushion glued to carcass
7 Self-closing system to retard drawer front 50mm (2in.) from closed position and pull it gently shut

ELEVATION, SCALE 1:50

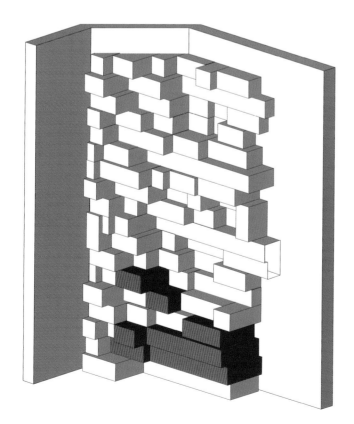

AXONOMETRIC

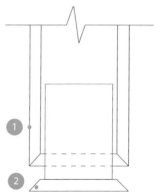

PLAN OF DRAWER, SCALE 1:10

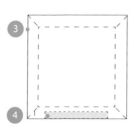

ELEVATION OF DRAWER FRONT,
SCALE 1:10

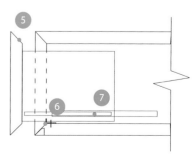

SECTION THROUGH DRAWER,
SCALE 1:10

SWAROVSKI, TOKYO
TOKUJIN YOSHIOKA

This store, on one of Swarovski's most prestigious sites, is intended to be the prototype for the company's interiors throughout the world. It is perhaps inevitable, and appropriate, that the brand's flagship store should have glass crystals both as an inspiration and a major component of the interior. While all the elements in the project will not necessarily be reproduced in all locations, the vocabulary and syntax for every smaller, or less prestigious, outlet is established here.

The upper half of the façade is composed of 1,500 stainless steel relief strips that are extrusions of the faceted section of a crystal. They reflect the changes of colour and movement of the street and sky throughout the day. The same strip components, but extruded in white acrylic, line the internal walls, suggesting the folds of a curtain and, with the predominantly white display units and furniture, make an appropriate backdrop for delicate and transparent merchandise.

Crystals, suspended in the double-height entrance space, represent the most literal response to the designer's concept of a 'crystal forest' and there are other, one-off, set pieces that are clearly inspired by waterfalls and ice formations. However it is the integration of crystals into more practical elements that provides their most original and ingenious applications. They are laid into the floor screed, like marble aggregate in terrazzo, to create randomly spaced highlights. Stair treads are constructed as trays to hold caches of crystals, which are lit from below by concealed lights, covered by glass tread plates and reflected in mirrored risers. The glass walls that surround the stairwell also reflect, more transparently, the highlighted facets of the randomly sized crystals.

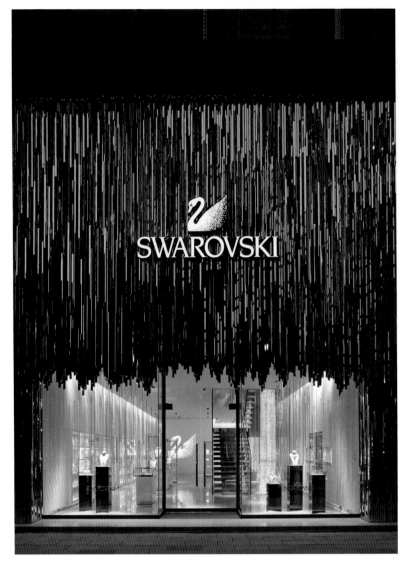

TOP
The upper external wall of faceted stainless steel rods reflects the light and activity of the city. The same moulding, in white acrylic, lines internal walls.

RIGHT
Illuminated treads and crystal sculpture glow through the filter of the glass enclosure on the upper floor.

OPPOSITE PAGE, TOP LEFT
Ground floor plan
1 Double-height crystal 'curtain'
2 Crystal 'cylinder'
3 Stair
4 Showcases
5 Recessed display cases
6 Counter
7 Sofa

OPPOSITE PAGE, TOP RIGHT
Glass and mirror-clad stair treads contain and reflect the light from LEDs buried amongst the crystals and reflected and diffused in the glass enclosure.

OPPOSITE PAGE, BOTTOM LEFT
The glass plate on the horizontal surface of the tread and the mirror on its vertical faces are supported and trimmed by fine brass sections.

OPPOSITE PAGE, BOTTOM RIGHT
The structure of the stair is conventional – welded steel with two central strings supporting treads that form shallow troughs to hold crystals and LED lights.

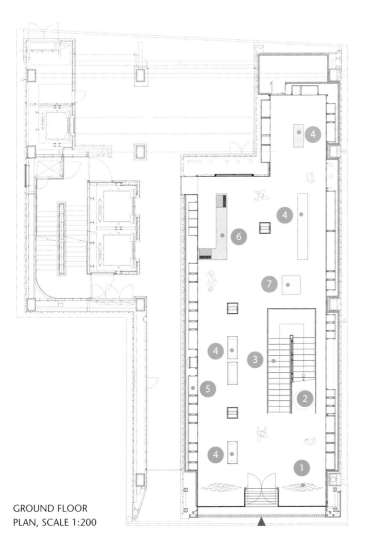

GROUND FLOOR
PLAN, SCALE 1:200

VERTU, TOKYO
KLEIN DYTHAM ARCHITECTURE

Vertu produce luxurious hand-crafted mobile telephones and this, their flagship store in Tokyo's most exclusive shopping district, reflects the quality of their product. The exterior's black aluminium cladding panels, gloss in the centre with two matt side strips, are screen-printed with the company logo. The central strip is returned into the interior to form a ceiling section that runs to the back wall where it transmutes into a floor-to-ceiling plasma screen that shows Vertu products.

The black and white palette of the ground floor reflects the colours of the brand identity and it is only on the upper floor, accessed by a stair decorated with an embossed version of the company logo, that monochromatic colour is relieved by red wall panels and carpet, perhaps to reward the eye in this windowless space. Both floors are otherwise united by horizontal convex wall panels that clad the side walls and by cubic black furniture.

There are two types of secure display cabinet. The first, a frameless glass box, sits on a black-stained wooden table base and contains trays of phones that slide out to give access to the products displayed. The second is a transparent acrylic screen, set at eye level within the white panelled walls, that runs the length of both side walls of the shop on the ground floor and on one side of the upper. The convex profile of this transparent panel matches that of the gloss white strips above and below it. Those immediately above and below it fold up and down to allow the tray carrying merchandise to slide open.

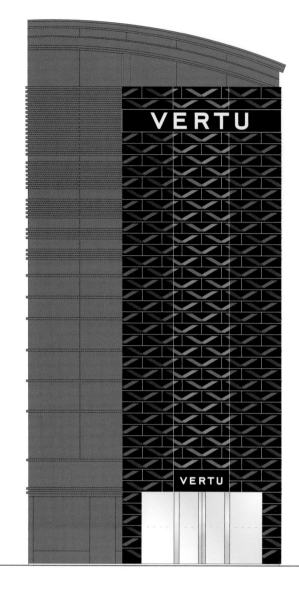

ABOVE RIGHT
Street façade
The screen-printed pattern on the cladding panels means that the precision of the drawn façade is replicated in the completed building.

BOTTOM RIGHT
The gloss centre strip is turned into the interior to form the central area of the ceiling.

BOTTOM MIDDLE
Red carpet and wall panels relieve the black and white palette in the upper, windowless, room.

OPPOSITE PAGE, TOP RIGHT
A gloss black aluminium strip is flanked by matt black side panels, all screen-printed with the brand logo.

OPPOSITE PAGE, BOTTOM RIGHT
The tabletop display cabinet: two trays slide open and shut.

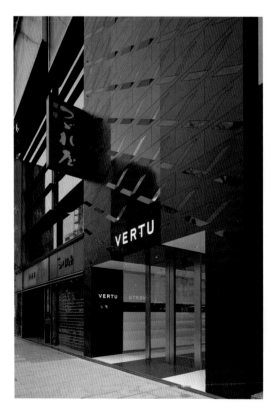

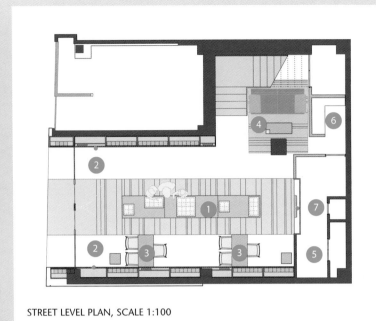

STREET LEVEL PLAN, SCALE 1:100

UPPER LEVEL PLAN, SCALE 1:100

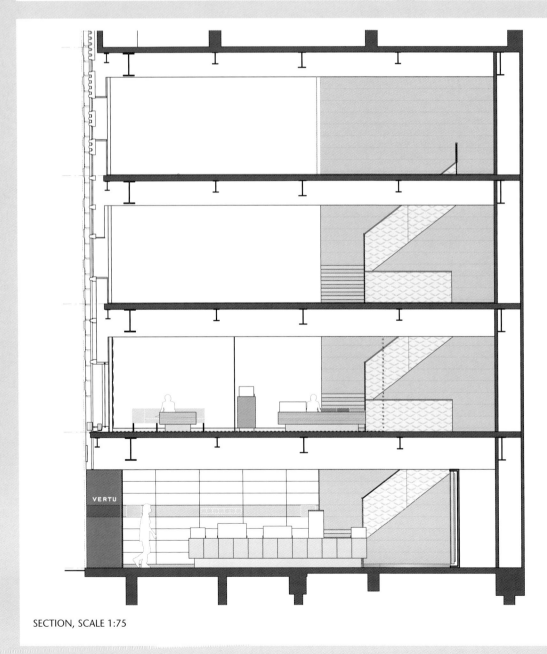

SECTION, SCALE 1:75

ABOVE LEFT
Street level plan
1 Central display
2 Feature wall
3 Consultation desk
4 Consultation sofa
5 Office
6 Wrapping counter
7 261cm (103in.) monitor

ABOVE RIGHT
Upper level plan
1 VIP room
2 Consultation table
3 Display wall
4 Display
5 Office

LEFT
Section
Cladding panels eliminate definition
of floor levels.

TOP RIGHT
Wall display – shut

BOTTOM RIGHT
Wall display – open

BELOW
Wall display detail
1 Top hinged white acrylic panel
2 Transparent tinted acrylic front to display cabinet
3 Bottom hinged white acrylic panel
4 Lock – accessed when panel 3 is lowered
5 White acrylic drawer front for storage
6 Double white acrylic drawer front for storage
7 Fixed white acrylic panels
8 Lighting for display cabinet
9 Display tray
10 Sliding drawer mechanism

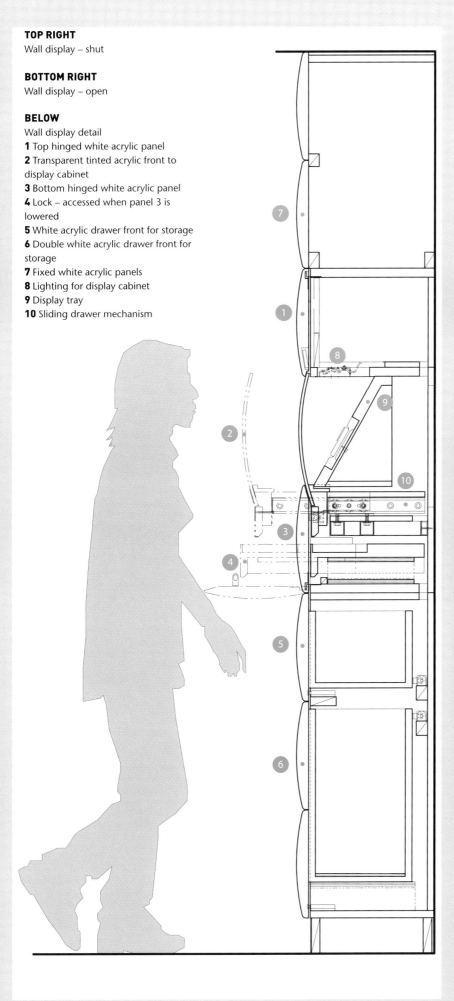

VOPNABÚRIÐ, REYKJAVIK
SRULI RECHT

Found objects may suggest a fictitious pedigree or confirm that the interior containing them belongs to its location. In this example the found objects clearly acknowledge the building's place in what was Reykjavik's fish-packing district, and the distinctive composition of objects for displaying and objects for display is defined by the specialist eye of the designer/shop owner, who also sees it as a place for continuing creative experimentation.

The bespoke font for the shop's sign is cut by high-pressure water jet from rusted roofing sheets. Its elegance and patina is counterpointed by the pristine yellow of the utilitarian façade. The letters appear to erode as the word progresses.

As the layers of accumulated finishes and equipment were stripped away from the building, the simple grandeur of structural concrete columns and beams became clear. Metal brackets and straps that were too substantial to remove were painted white to reduce their presence. Well-worn, ceiling-mounted timbers, used as supports for light fittings, were left unpainted, to make a link to the recovered timbers below.

The gnarled wooden stacking frames and steel wheeled trolleys used as storage and display elements also clearly belong to the past of the building shell. A more delicate layering of objects is generated by the designer's involvement with clothing production. Utilitarian hanging rails become frames for screens of non-woven interfacing.

Cardboard storage boxes also provide the raw material for furniture-making experiments. The counter and display case exploits the ease with which the material may be cut to create a comparatively rigid interlocking structure and to make circles that respond to the rounded corners of the original cardboard boxes.

TOP RIGHT
The shop's name is cut from rusted tin roofing sheets by high-pressure water jet.

MIDDLE RIGHT
Interlocking cardboard planes can achieve the rigidity needed to produce viable pieces of simple furniture.

BOTTOM RIGHT
Cardboard sheet has some of the roughness of the found objects. Interfacing fabric has visual affinity with the worn timber stacking.

OPPOSITE PAGE
The shell was stripped back to its essential structure and reinhabited with found objects, new composite objects – here a hanging rail frame for an interfacing screen – and set piece displays.

CLOTHING

ALL SAINTS, CARDIFF
BRINKWORTH

Target customers for this clothes chain are young, with a taste for street fashion, and the designers, who have been responsible for all the brand's interiors, look for building shells with existing elements sympathetic to that aesthetic. This tends to favour the selection of older, utilitarian building shells and, while it is often difficult to investigate the potential of such spaces before final acquisition of a site, accurate conclusions can usually be drawn about their potential from the clues offered by exterior construction and a knowledge of local building practices.

In a building of any age, after successive layers of finishes have been peeled back, it is likely that characterful materials and elements will be uncovered that may be incorporated into the brand formula. But where good business sense suggests location in a modern shopping mall that offers no inherent idiosyncrasies, the designers use theatrical set builders to make plaster casts of sections of brick walls, which are screwed to plywood wall linings and 'distressed' using paint techniques. Non-structural steel columns and beams are often added to underpin the illusion of industrial archaeology, and to subdivide areas within the bland box of a mall unit.

In this example the excavation process yielded walls and floor areas of considerable character. However, the branding element in all recent All Saints interiors is the dense lining of the street frontages with redundant sewing machines that, as they have been replaced by digital manufacturing techniques, have become symbols of less impersonal production methods. The worn timber machine bases are fixed to socket-jointed tubular poles. Here, as in all the brand's units, whether in old buildings or new, bespoke display and light fittings are assembled using materials and techniques that suggest crude manufacturing processes and expedient manual assembly rather than smooth machine production.

RIGHT
While retaining the visual identity of their particular model, the tightly packed machines become a single light filter.

FAR RIGHT
Decayed and distressed brickwork and crudely patched fragments of original flooring create an appropriate context for the merchandise.

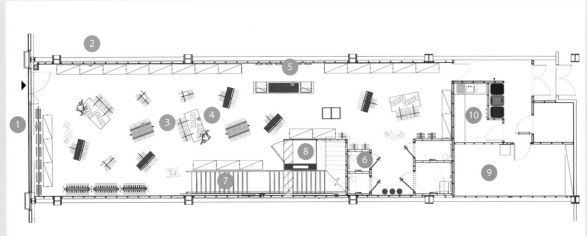

GROUND FLOOR PLAN, SCALE 1:200

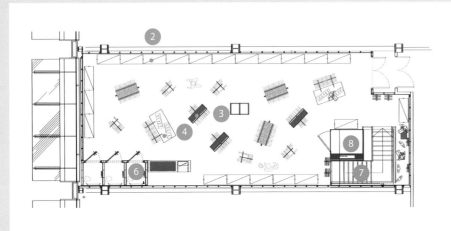

FIRST FLOOR PLAN, SCALE 1:200

LEFT & MIDDLE

Plans

1 Sewing machine display
2 Hanging rails with shelves above
3 Hanging rails
4 Display tables
5 Counter
6 Changing cubicles
7 Stair
8 Lift
9 Store
10 Staff

BOTTOM

A virtue is made of the most basic nuts and bolts but the original enamelling of the sewing machines' metal bases introduces delicate decoration.

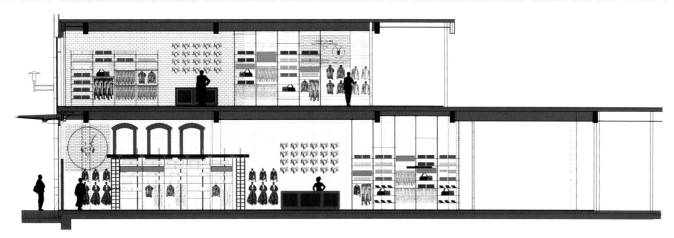

ELEVATION, SCALE 1:200

ABOVE
Elevation
Intense surface texture is evident even in the drawing.

RIGHT
The pattern and texture of reclaimed materials establish the character of the interior.

BELOW RIGHT
New bespoke light fittings use materials and assembly techniques that suggest obsolete industrial processes.

ANTONIOS MARKOS, ATHENS
GONZALEZ HAASE

The building shell, on the ground and first floors of a corner site, was stripped back to its structural elements: floors, walls, columns, beams and a staircase. The new interior was created by the insertion of a number of faceted components – conceived and resolved on computer and manufactured by CNC (computer numerical control) tools, which are capable of realizing physically complex three-dimensional forms digitally generated. Because of the precision with which it may be worked, MDF is used for the faceted units. Spray painting, which matches the colour of the corrugated plastic sheets used for changing cubicle walls, eliminates all trace of joints.

A basic three-dimensional display module was aggregated in various configurations to form 'islands' that, while sharing a generic angled profile, are clearly dissimilar in overall form so that each is distinctive enough to suggest that it belongs only to its particular location. The scale of each aggregation also suggests a permanent entity, which may be added to using the same basic component and method of production, creating an impression of organic growth that is also suggested by the irregular lengths and angles of the wall-mounted chrome clothes-hanging bars.

CNC techniques also made possible the intricate faceted mirrored form that clings to the external corner of the walls around the stairwell, and the more visually delicate construction of the changing rooms, in which matt, translucent, light grey acrylic panels, slightly corrugated on their edges for extra rigidity, are screwed to a structure of chrome tubes. The interlocking of sheets, which exposes the thinness of the material, demonstrates fragility in contrast to the solidity of the MDF floor pieces.

ABOVE
A faceted mirror clings to the corner of the stair enclosure, creating a kaleidoscopic image of the interior.

RIGHT
Intricately faceted display plinths and complex hanging rails contrast with the simplicity of the existing shell. The precision of CNC production allows high and low junctions on adjacent units to line through exactly.

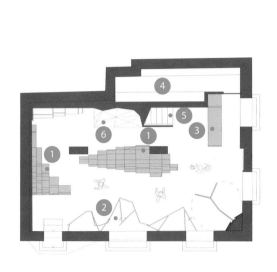

LOWER LEVEL PLAN, SCALE 1:200

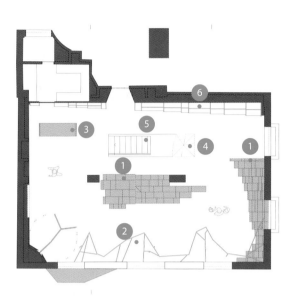

UPPER LEVEL PLAN, SCALE 1:200

RIGHT
CNC manufacture allows dimensions to be adapted to suit different items of merchandise.

BELOW RIGHT
Mirrored faces, again cut with extreme precision, further complicate the perceived form of the plinths.

OPPOSITE PAGE, TOP
Lower level plan
1 Faceted display unit
2 Wall-mounted hanging rails
3 Counter
4 Storage
5 Stair
6 Faceted mirror

Upper level plan
1 Faceted display unit
2 Wall-mounted hanging rails
3 Counter
4 Faceted mirror
5 Stair
6 Shelving

OPPOSITE PAGE, BOTTOM LEFT
Changing cubicles are more visually fragile but the creasing of acrylic panels and bunching of the curtain have an affinity with the faceted surfaces of display plinths.

OPPOSITE PAGE, BOTTOM RIGHT
CNC cutting allows perfect alignment of interlocking sheets and delicate radiusing of corners.

ARMANI,
NEW YORK
FUKSAS

The interior is dominated by two staircases, one leading to basement level, one to the two upper floors. Both are conceived as ribbons that twist through the volumes as if continuously and organically evolving. The designers suggest that they represent vortices off which floor layouts and display elements spin.

The complexity of their forms makes it impossible to recognize formal geometries within them, and that complexity is increased when the ribbons that serve as handrails and balustrades split and spin off above head height to confound any expectation of them as merely utilitarian elements. The comparatively solid enclosures created by these writhing ribbons separate customers from the more familiar shopping activities of display and sales that are then freshly encountered when they emerge on each floor from the isolation of the vortex.

The elements of both stairs were constructed on a structural skeleton of welded rolled-steel tubes. The basic three-dimensional form was established by 168mm (6⅝in)-diameter horizontal and 127mm (5in.)-diameter vertical tubes and stiffened with 8mm (¼in.) steel plate. This skeleton was then covered with an expanded metal lath onto which 20mm (¾in.) of glass-reinforced concrete was sprayed to give a smooth monolithic finish that flows seamlessly between levels. The visual integrity of the upward-sweeping ribbons is consolidated by the open treads, of 6mm (¼in.) folded steel plate, that erode the solidity of the horizontals and allow the vertical planes to be perceived as continuous elements.

On upper levels curved walls spin off from the stair vortex, defining dedicated sales areas and masking service and storage spaces. Smooth plastic curves define display furniture and cash desks. Concealed light sources accentuate form and movement.

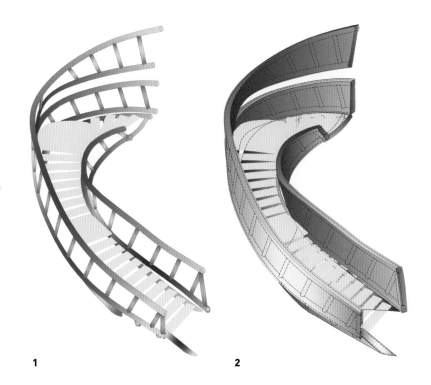

1   2

3

THIS PAGE
1 Tubular skeleton (prefabricated in Italy).
2 Skeleton stiffened by steel plate (shown in grey).
3 Structure covered in expanded metal lath and glass-reinforced concrete.

OPPOSITE PAGE, TOP
The elements of the stair fragment. Artificial lighting creates an internalized environment.

OPPOSITE PAGE, BOTTOM LEFT
Open risers undermine the solidity of the horizontal planes.

OPPOSITE PAGE, BOTTOM RIGHT
The stair becomes the focal and pivotal element on each floor.

RIGHT

Ground floor plan
1 Stair to basement
2 Stair to upper floors
3 Lifts
4 Display and sales
5 Entrance
6 Other tenants

MIDDLE

Third floor plan
1 Stair
2 Lifts
3 Restaurant and bar
4 Display and sales
5 Service areas

BELOW

Elevation
The stair to the basement introduces the
theme that evolves on the upper floors.

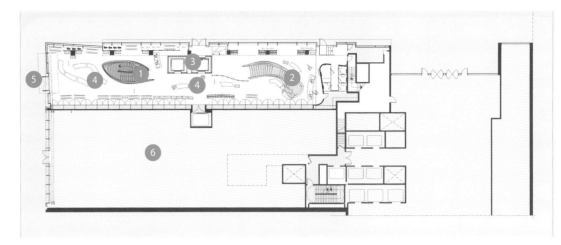

GROUND FLOOR PLAN, SCALE 1:200

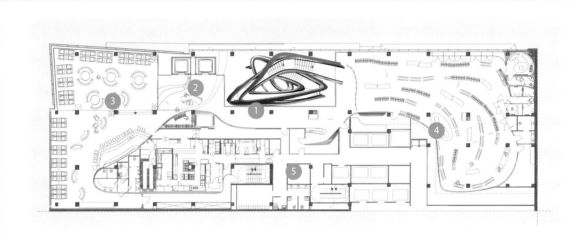

THIRD FLOOR PLAN, SCALE 1:200

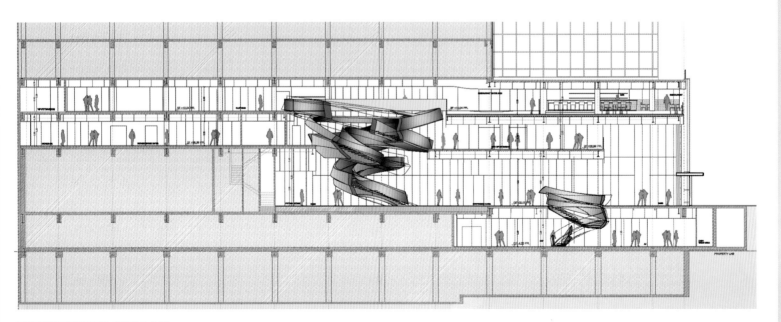

EAST/WEST SECTION, SCALE 1: 150

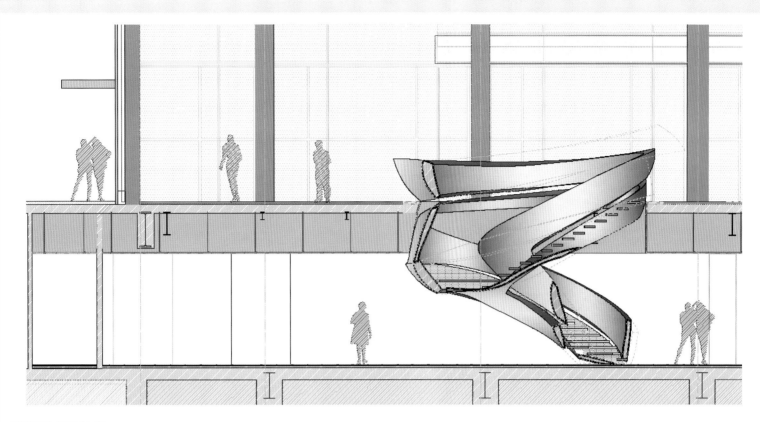

SECTION, SCALE 1:50

ABOVE
Section
Freeform balustrades mask the regular
geometry of treads and risers.

BELOW
The soaring balustrades envelop and
dwarf customers.

AYRES,
BUENOS AIRES
DIEGUEZ FRIDMAN ARQUITECTOS & ASOCIADOS

The interior sets out to replicate the experience of being in an external urban space, to create an equivalent of the variety of form, the continually changing views, the unexpected incidents encountered in the density and complexity of a city. Customers moving through the circulation spaces gaze at mannequins scattered through the sales zones as they would at strangers glimpsed across a city space.

The complexity of the visual experience is revealed as customers progress through the store on a sequence of ramps and stairs that form an armature around which spaces for display, changing rooms and sales counters are organized. The proliferation of planes, both angled and inclined, complicate and confuse perception of the whole and suggest a volume much bigger than it is.

Ramps and stairs are conceived as smooth, bright white objects unfolding in curves and angles within the dark textured box that is defined by floors, walls and ceilings. The textures of the concrete screed floor and the heavy timber steps connecting minor changes of level suggest something organic.

The smooth white surfaces are achieved by a combination of materials. The floor is white plastic laminate sheet. Pliable white plastic fabric stretched over a skeleton frame covers less vulnerable planes, like the soffits and sides of ramps and stairs. The heights and angles of the upper and lower edges of balustrades vary to increase abstraction and camouflage the necessarily regular geometry of stairs, ramps and handrails. Each tread rests separately on a continuous sloping plane, so that the perception of continuous sloping surfaces is maintained throughout the circulation zone.

ABOVE RIGHT
Strong white diagonals float against the dark planes of walls and ceiling.

RIGHT
The pure white forms of the circulation elements, 'Barrisol' white stretch fabric over an aluminium frame, unwind through the darker, rougher textured sales areas.

OPPOSITE PAGE
Customers moving through the circulation zones catch glimpses of the other world of mannequins.

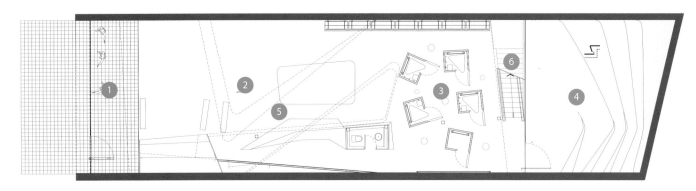

LOWER LEVELS PLAN, SCALE 1:200

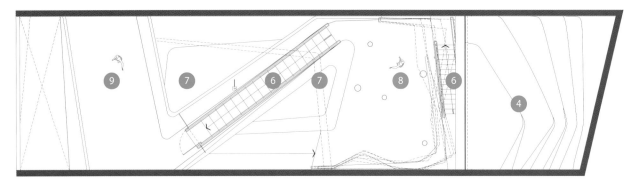

UPPER LEVELS PLAN, SCALE 1:200

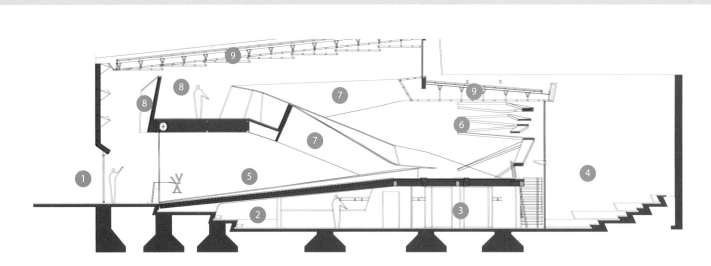

SECTION, SCALE 1:200

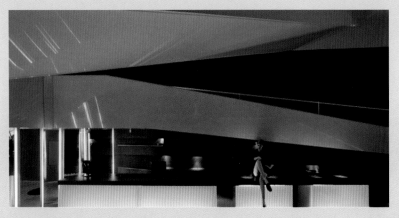

LEFT
The minimal tubular handrail maintains
the regulatory balustrade height and lets
the solid plane follow an alternative angle.

TOP
Lower and upper levels plans
1 Glazed entrance wall
2 Lower display and sales area
3 Changing rooms
4 External courtyard
5 Ramp 1:10 gradient
6 Stairs
7 Voids

8 Intermediate level
9 Highest level

MIDDLE
Section
1 Glazed entrance wall
2 Lower display and sales area
3 Changing rooms
4 External courtyard
5 Ramp 1:10 gradient
6 Intermediate display area
7 Stretch fabric over aluminum frame
8 Highest floor area
9 Suspended ceiling

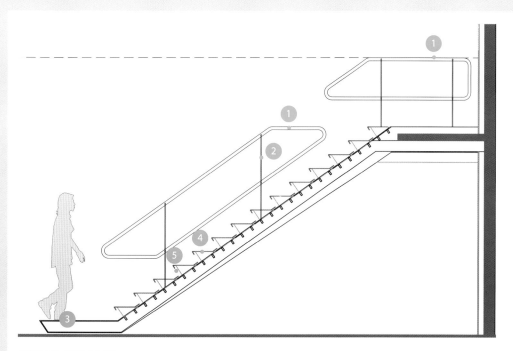

SECTION, SCALE 1:50

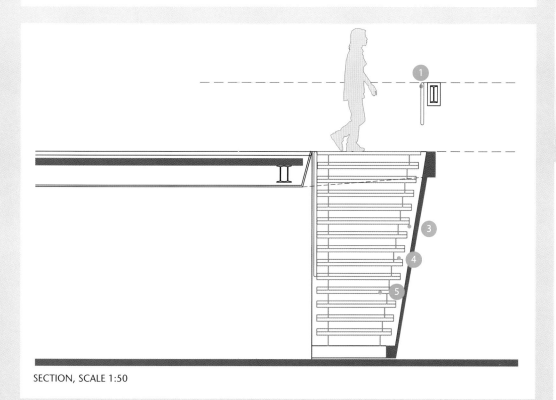

SECTION, SCALE 1:50

TOP LEFT & ABOVE
Section through typical stair flight. The
width of the stair varies along the length
of the flight.
1 40mm (1⅝in.)-diameter tubular
steel handrail
2 12mm (½in.) supporting rod
3 30mm (1³⁄₁₆in.) mechanically polished
granolithic screed poured in situ
4 5mm (³⁄₁₆in.) steel plate step
5 6mm (¼in.) steel support for step

TOP RIGHT
Stair treads are designed to be visually
distinct from the continuous sloping
plane that supports them.

BOTTOM RIGHT
Detail: steps on ground floor level
1 Polished concrete floor screed
2 Precast concrete riser with embedded
LED light
3 In situ concrete
4 Embedded LED light

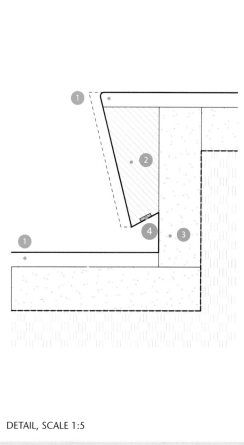

DETAIL, SCALE 1:5

BASTARD,
MILAN
STUDIOMETRICO

Comvert was founded by skate- and snow boarders, to design, manufacture and distribute clothing for their sports under the brand name Bastard. Studiometrico were asked to find and design their new headquarters building, and chose the old Cinema Istria. They decided on a design strategy that would support Comvert's informal, collaborative working methods. The idiosyncrasies of the original building set particular problems that were crucial in development of the solution.

The retail sales area occupies what was the main entrance to the cinema. The opportunity for Comvert staff, all of whom work one day a month in the shop, to talk to customers was seen to be as important as selling. The display structures and cash desks are manufactured from timbers left over from the building of the office. The fitting rooms are remnants from the construction of the Bowl.

Administration is housed in the former semicircular foyer. A new larch platform provides a level working surface on top of the original sloping marble floor and three storage elements provide some privacy within what is now a principal circulation area.

The design department is located on the old balcony. A new steel structure, fixed to the existing concrete beams, supports wooden platforms that create terraces providing clearly defined working areas without inhibiting employee communication. The lower steps of the balcony are unmodified to make a showroom space for visiting wholesale buyers and areas for fashion shows, informal meetings and recreation.

The dominant element within the old auditorium is the Bastard Bowl, perched on top of two floors of warehousing with a structure of glued laminate beams and curved steel posts.

TOP RIGHT
In the original foyer the marble floor, stairs, handrails and column-mounted light fittings remain. The raised platform for the office corrects the slight slope of the floor and three storage units provide some privacy.

MIDDLE RIGHT
At the lowest levels of the balcony, the original steps are retained to create a variety of flexible spaces for wholesale customers, staff meetings and relaxation.

BOTTOM RIGHT
Furniture is detailed to deal with the idiosyncrasies of the cinema shell.

OPPOSITE PAGE, TOP
Timber terraces rest on the former stepped balcony to make well-defined work spaces without inhibiting interaction. Shelves and desks give stability to the larch boarding of the balustrades.

OPPOSITE PAGE, BOTTOM
Wheeled units sit on the original marble floor. The vertical tubes are connected to both the top and bottom of the wooden bases to provide stability.

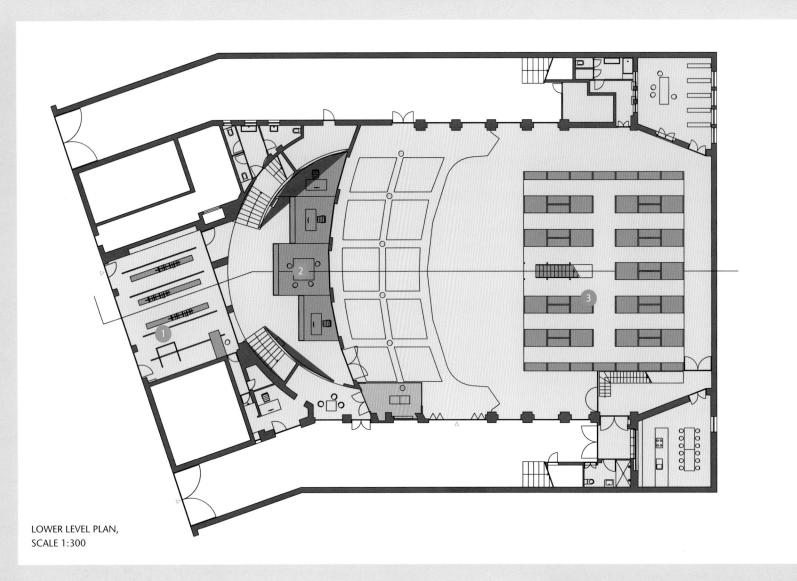

LOWER LEVEL PLAN,
SCALE 1:300

ABOVE
Lower level plan
1 Shop
2 Office
3 Warehousing

LEFT
Upper level plan
1 Design studio
2 Meeting, wholesale display, catwalk
3 Skateboard bowl

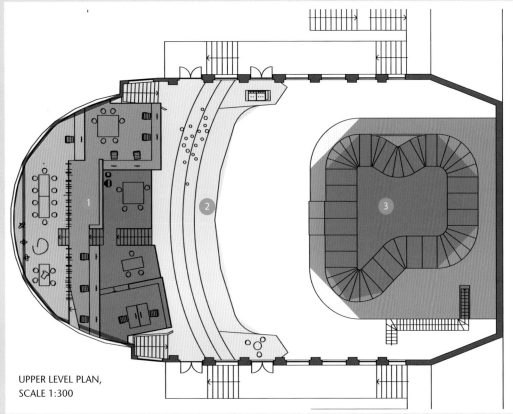

UPPER LEVEL PLAN,
SCALE 1:300

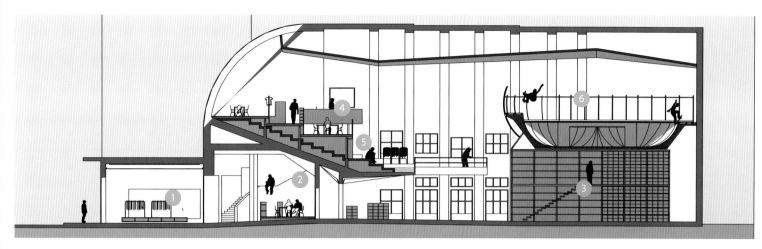

SECTION, SCALE 1:300

ABOVE
Section
1 Shop
2 Office
3 Warehousing
4 Design studio
5 Meeting, wholesale display, catwalk
6 Skateboard bowl

BELOW
Two floors of warehousing sit
below the skateboarding bowl,
which sits level with the design
department.

RIGHT

The structure that supports the Bowl is contained within the warehouse structure.

BOTTOM RIGHT

Section through edge of bowl

1 Continuous steel profile 50 x 4 mm
2 Metal mesh
3 Curved steel beam
4 Continuous steel profile 80 x 4 mm
5 Channel steel element 45 x 45 x 2 mm
6 Steel plate 50 x 8 x 150 mm
7 Steel plate 50 x 4 x 150 mm
8 Steel plate 80 x 8 x 150 mm
9 Channel steel profile 100 x 100 x10mm
10 10 bolts
11 Steel beam
12 Timber cross rib to support plywood sheets
13 Laminated timber ribs
14 46 mm long channel steel element

Components are bolted together

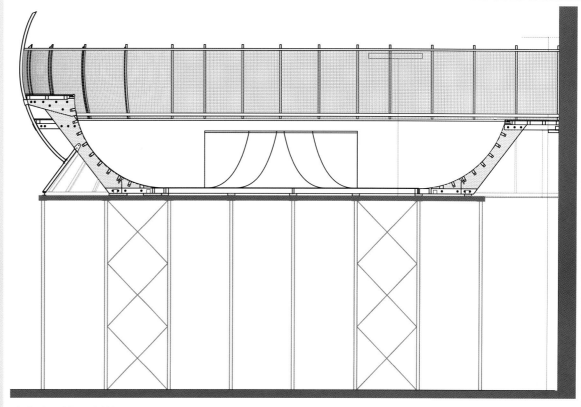

SECTION, SCALE 1:100

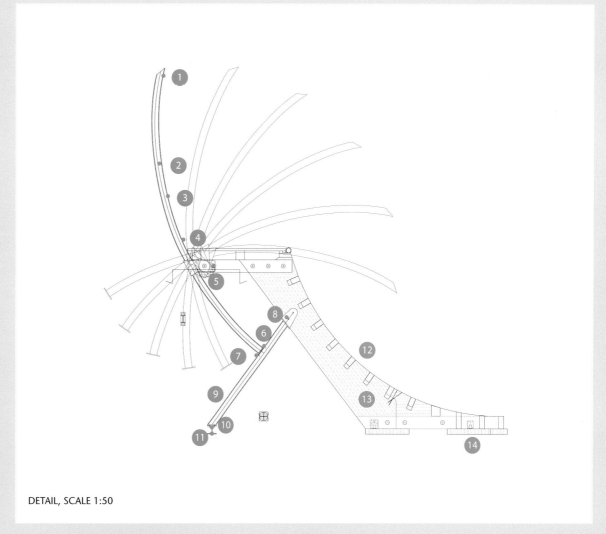

DETAIL, SCALE 1:50

BASTYAN, LONDON
BRINKWORTH

Bastyan offers women, in a target group aged over 30 and with significant disposable income, a coherently edited collection of clothing and accessories. The interior sets out to suggest an appropriate elegance and quality. The brand operates primarily as a concession outlet within department stores and its interiors must solve the problems facing all such operations – of defining territory, providing adequate display and storage opportunities without four perimeter walls, and establishing a presence amongst the visual confusion created by competing outlets.

The Bastyan solution is a muted materials palette of blue-stained oak for shelves and framing with patinated metal trimmings, rails and fixings. Brand presence is signalled by a storage and display unit that is, in effect, a rear wall carrying the Bastyan name, and its territory is marked out by the tables, plinths and hanging rails that sit just far enough in from the 'demise' line, the boundary of rented floor space, to ensure that customers can circulate solely within the parameters of Bastyan space.

The amount of merchandise displayed on the rear wall is limited to allow the elements that identify the brand to assert themselves. Apart from three crucial garments that are front hung, the rest are discreetly stored at low level. The remainder of the wall is subdivided to suggest small, pivoting window panes, each embossed with the Bastyan logo, hinting at grander windows that might open to an exterior. The floor-mounted units share refinement of angles, curves and projections that, with solidity of construction, underpin the implication of product quality. As does the sparse presentation – the front-hanging display, restricted to the few spaces on the rear wall not occupied by the 'windows' and the precise allocation of merchandise within the subdivisions of tabletops.

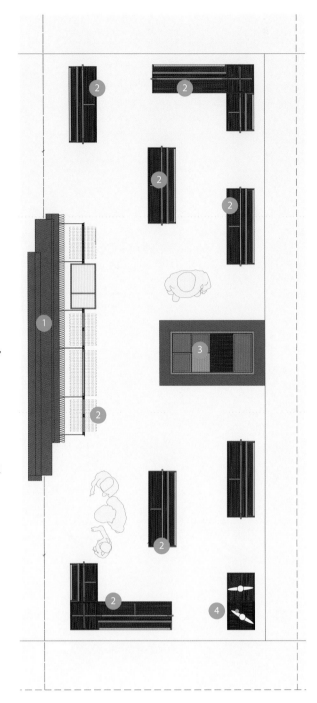

PLAN, SCALE 1:50

ABOVE
Plan
1 Rear display wall
2 Floor hanging
3 Display table
4 Mannequin plinth

OPPOSITE PAGE
All elements share a restrained palette of blue-stained oak with patinated steel and brass trimmings.

BASTYAN

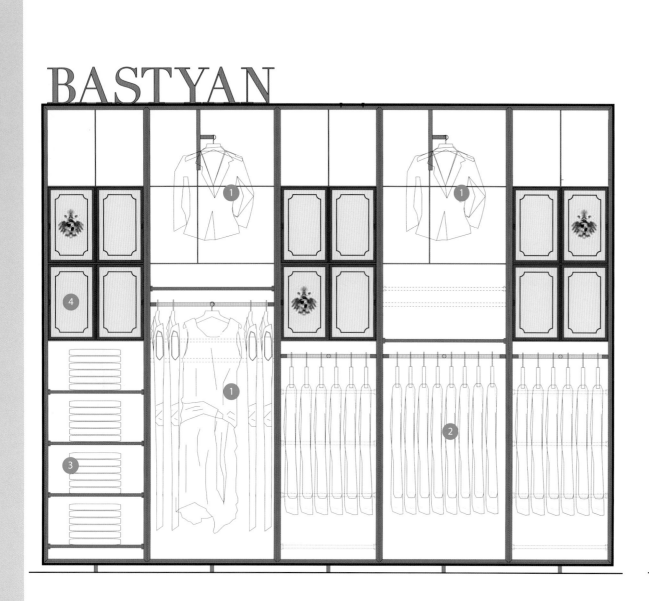

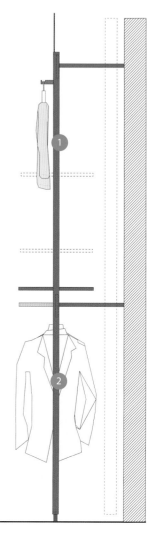

ELEVATION, SCALE 1:20

END ELEVATION

ABOVE
Rear display wall – front
and side elevations
1 Front hanging
2 Side hanging
3 Shelves
4 'Windows'

OPPOSITE PAGE, TOP
Mid-floor hanging: the angled wooden
frame is braced by the hanging rail
and the bent tube connecting it to the
wooden base plate.

OPPOSITE PAGE, BOTTOM
Mid-floor hanging: the projecting
brass tube that ends the hanging rail is
grooved to hold the hanger for holding
front-facing garments in position.
1 Wooden frame
2 Tubular hanging rail
3 Bracing tube
4 Brass inlay strip
5 Brass end piece

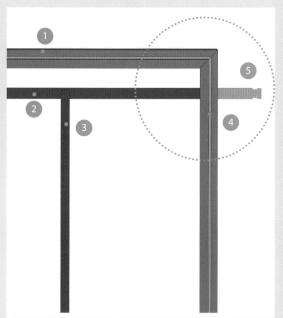

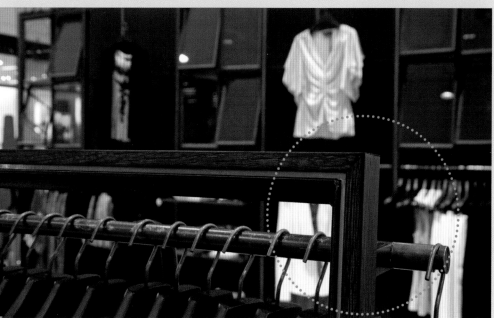

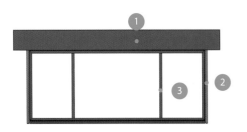

FRONT ELEVATION, SCALE 1:20

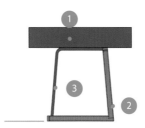

SIDE ELEVATION, SCALE 1:20

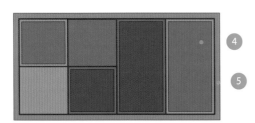

PLAN, SCALE 1:20

ABOVE
The table uses the same structural and detailing principles as the hanging units.

LEFT
Elevations and plan of table
1 Blue oak edge with mitred corners
2 Blue oak frame with radius edges and mitred corners
3 Mild steel tube to brace tabletop and blue oak base

Plan
4 Trays and boxes for display items.
5 Raised edges

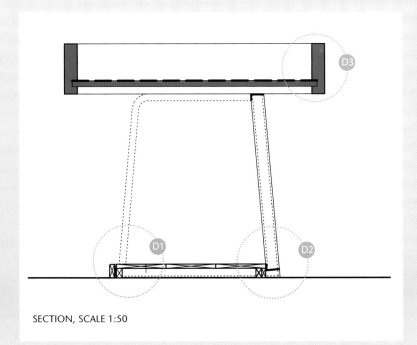

SECTION, SCALE 1:50

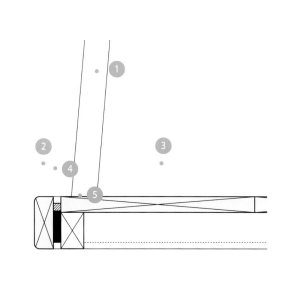

DETAIL 1, SCALE 1:5

ABOVE AND RIGHT
Section through table and related details
Detail 1
1 20mm (¾in.) blue/black mild steel tube mechanically fixed to brass tube and blue oak base
2 40 x 15mm (1⅝ x ⅝in.) blue oak frame with radius edges and mitred corners
3 Blue oak base on wooden stud frame.
4 6 x 6mm (¼ x ¼in.) antique brass strip set back 5mm (³⁄₁₆in.) from face of frame, clamped between steel sections on mild steel packing piece
5 Frame
Detail 2
6 40 x 15mm (1⅝ x ⅝in.) blue oak frame with radius edges and mitred junctions
7 Blue-black 40 x 20 x 3mm (1⅝ x ¾ x ⅛in.) mild steel 'L' section with mitred edge corners

8 Blue-black oak base on wooden stud frame
9 Frame
Detail 3
10 18mm (¾in.) blue oak veneered MDF.
11 Blue oak edge pieces
12 Blue-black 40 x 20 x 3mm (1⅝ x ¾ x ⅛in.) mild steel 'L' section with mitred edge junctions
13 40 x 15mm (1⅝ x ⅝in.) blue oak frame with radius edges and mitred junctions

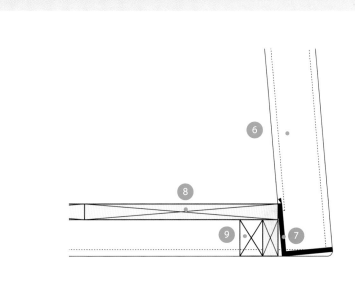

DETAIL 2, SCALE 1:5

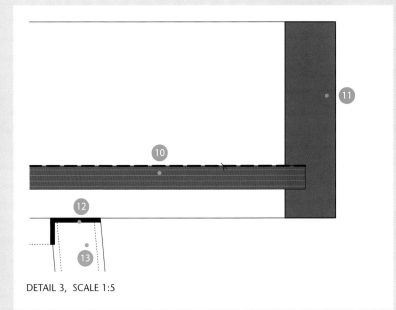

DETAIL 3, SCALE 1:5

BOXFRESH, LONDON
BRINKWORTH

The shapes and configurations of the white board elements on walls and floors are obviously inspired by those found in a deconstructed cardboard box. While there is a current vogue for assembling interiors that are expected to have a short lifespan and gentle usage from cut and folded sheets of cardboard, the material has not the solidity necessary for a longer period of hard use, nor can it be folded or bent with precision.

For this project the designers chose to use Dibond, a 3mm (⅛in.) thick but light and very rigid composite sheet consisting of a polyethylene core sandwiched between two aluminium sheets, which can be cut and bent precisely. They collaborated with a specialist fabricator to evolve and produce a series of elements that share, with origami, principles of production and assembly. The flat Dibond sheets are cut and creased to make the slits and folds necessary to assemble the various wall and floor elements. Forms were partly determined by an ambition to minimize wastage. Three-dimensional profiles increased the carrying capacity of shelves. All wall panels were supported on battens and finished at least 20mm (¾in.) off the wall to cope with irregularities and changes in surface planes.

The smooth, flat Dibond provided an extreme contrast to the textures of the reclaimed brickwork, and a base for text. Some of the larger logos were produced by 'half routing' or cutting halfway into the sheet to expose its black core.

Key Clamp, a refined scaffolding system suitable for permanent installations, was used for handrails and hanging rails, and for reinforcing those Dibond structures required to support heavy loads. Its matt steel finish aligned it visually with the surface-mounted pipework and electrical conduit.

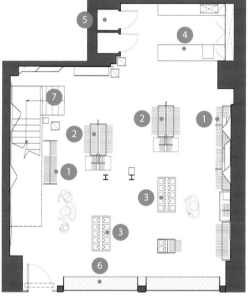

GROUND FLOOR PLAN, SCALE 1:100

TOP RIGHT
The cut sheet may be folded and opened out to make text panels and light deflectors. Key Clamp provides hanging rails strong enough to carry dense side hanging.

OPPOSITE PAGE
The Dibond sheet can also be folded to make shelves, set forward on timber battens to cope with changes in wall planes and wrapped around bulkheads. The proprietary Key Clamp balustrade matches the steel of the surface-mounted electrical conduits and pipework.

RIGHT
Ground floor plan
1 Wall-hung display
2 Floor-mounted display
3 Table display
4 Counter
5 Changing cubicles
6 Window display
7 Stair up

First floor plan
1 Wall-hung display
2 Floor-mounted display
3 Table display
4 Changing cubicles
5 Stair down

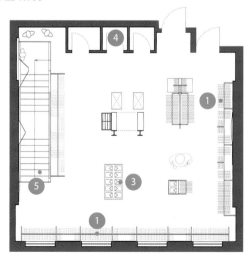

FIRST FLOOR PLAN, SCALE 1:100

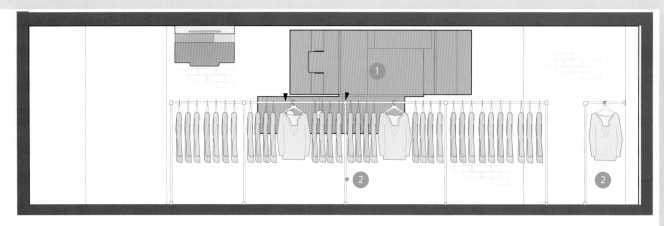

ELEVATION , UPPER FLOOR, SCALE 1:50

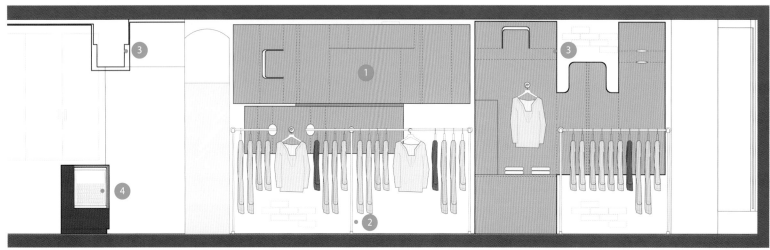

ELEVATION, GROUND FLOOR, SCALE 1:50

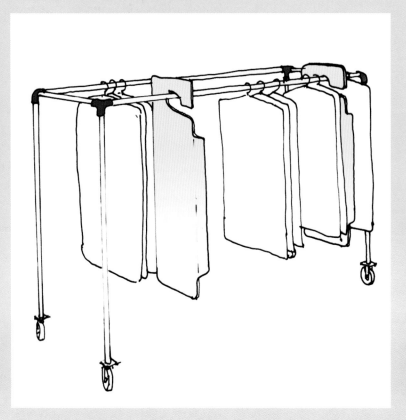

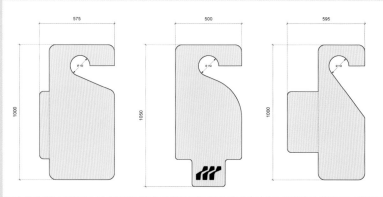

ABOVE TOP
Elevation – upper floor
1 Dibond board fixed to timber battens on original brickwork
2 Key Clamp framing passes through Dibond and is fixed directly to brickwork

ABOVE MIDDLE
Elevation – ground floor
1 Dibond board fixed to timber battens on original brickwork
2 Key Clamp framing passes through Dibond and is fixed directly to brickwork
3 Dibond-clad downstands fixed to original ceiling
4 Counter

ABOVE BOTTOM
Profile variations for separating boards.

LEFT
Dibond boards, hung on Key Clamp rails, separate merchandise.

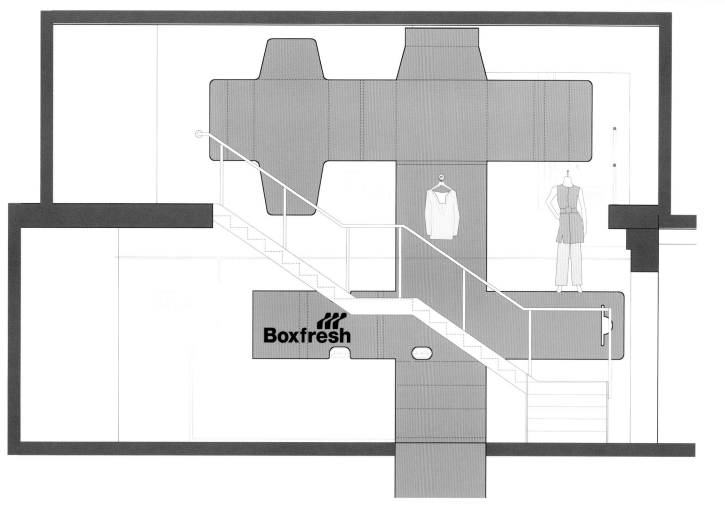

ELEVATION, SCALE 1:50

ABOVE
The cut Dibond board, shown grey, is folded along the black lines to form the three dimensional element shown below right.

RIGHT
The precut Dibond aluminium sheet, which obviously refers to the shapes of unassembled boxes, may be folded to create decorative and utilitarian forms. Its smoothness provides a counterpoint to the original stripped brickwork.

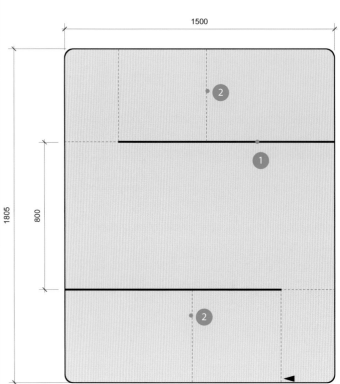

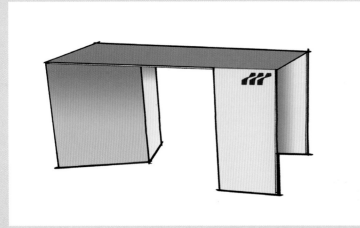

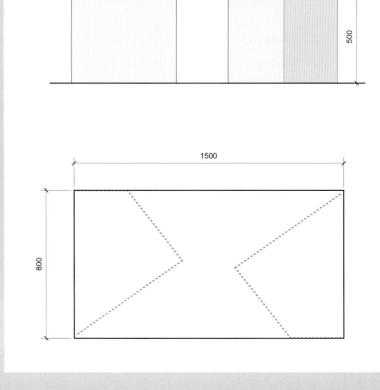

TOP
Mid-floor pieces use the same construction principles as wall elements; cut and folded Dimond board with Key Clamp to take heavier loads.

ABOVE
The folding pattern indicates where the logo should be printed on the flat sheet.

RIGHT
The standard Dimond sheet is cut, along the black lines, and folded on the red to make the low display table. Exposed corners are rounded to prevent damage to units and injury to customers.
1 Line of cut
2 Line of fold

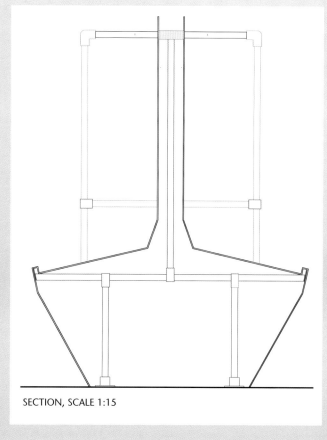

SECTION, SCALE 1:15

ABOVE
The Dibond board, supported on Key Clamp, provides a backdrop for side- and front-hung garments and an inclined display shelf.
(See also photograph on the left).

ABOVE RIGHT
Section through the end display shelf. Double sheets provide shelving on both faces.

RIGHT
The single board that acts as a division between the two faces of the unit is treaded on to the cross tubes that connect the two hanging rails.
1 Dibond board, single sheet
2 Exposed frame
3 Concealed frame between doubled shelf sheets

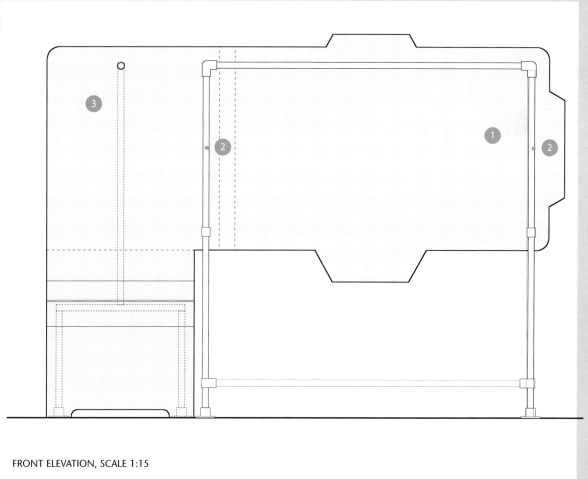

FRONT ELEVATION, SCALE 1:15

DOUBLE OO '96,
FUKUOKA
CASE-REAL

The simplicity of the interior is signalled at the entrance by the glass wall that vanishes, without any visible frame, into the horizontal and vertical planes that surround it, by the floor-to-ceiling door, also without visible framing, and by the shop's name, which is discreetly incised on the letter box.

The façade is skewed so that it makes a right-angled junction with the wall separating the main sales floor from the secondary area along the side window, facing onto the pedestrian passageway. This short length of straight wall evolves into a curve that widens out to meet the indent on the rear wall, making space for an office, storage room, lavatory and changing cubicles. A step to the changing rooms, of waxed concrete to match the floor, runs to and wraps around the end wall to become a plinth for shoes and accessories.

The ceiling plane becomes a second curve bending to meet the clothes display cabinets on the long side wall. A deep fascia conceals the hanging rail and the light source that washes up to dramatize the curve.

The vertical and horizontal curves reinforce the designer's idea of the interior as a cave and the omission of a skirting emphasizes the monumentality of the curved wall, which is given an implied thickness by the recesses within the window zone that contain wooden display cabinets. These cabinets are detailed to sit independently on and in the wall so that they become intermediaries between the seeming permanence of the curved elements and the transience of the merchandise.

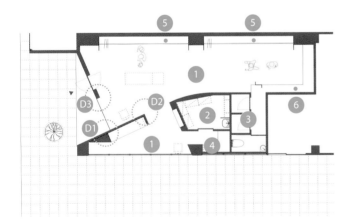

PLAN, SCALE 1:200

ABOVE
1 Sales area
2 Store
3 Changing cubicles
4 Office
5 Hanging rails
6 Plinth

RIGHT
The right-angled wall evolves into a curve, behind which are the service areas. The ceiling makes the second curved plane.

LEFT
A mirror at plinth level reflects the ceiling that curves behind the hanging cabinets.

BELOW LEFT
The letter box is finished with the same textured sheet material as the door and walls. The slot around it frames the incised name of the shop.

BELOW
The angled wall makes a display zone to the pedestrian area that is accessible to customers.

BELOW RIGHT
The letter box detail.

BELOW

Detail D1
1 Plasterboard
2 Timber strip
3 Smooth render (to match exterior) on plasterboard
4 Metal stud frame
5 Metal fixing bracket

RIGHT

Detail D2
1 Interior
2 Exterior
3 Plasterboard
4 Smooth render
5 External quality cladding board
6 Metal frame
7 Glass
8 Clear film
9 Plasterboard
10 Metal strip
11 Textured external cladding
12 Metal stud Frame

BOTTOM RIGHT

Detail D3
1 Existing structure
2 Metal fixing bracket
3 Timber strip
4 External quality cladding board
5 Smooth render
6 Metal stud frame

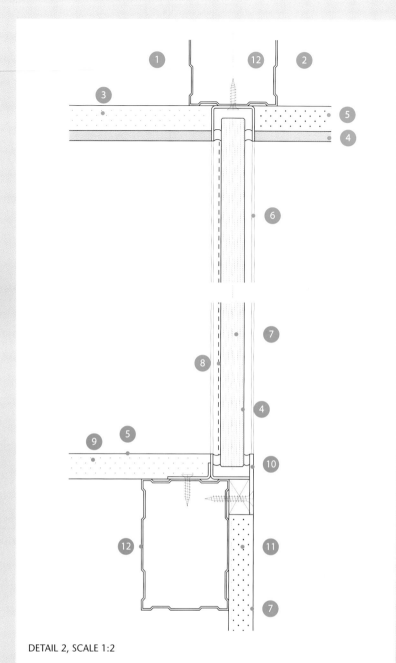

DETAIL 2, SCALE 1:2

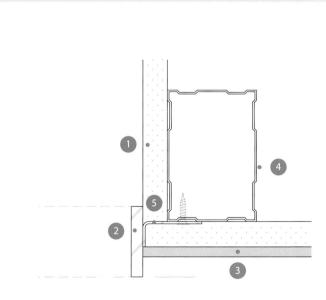

DETAIL 1, SCALE 1:2

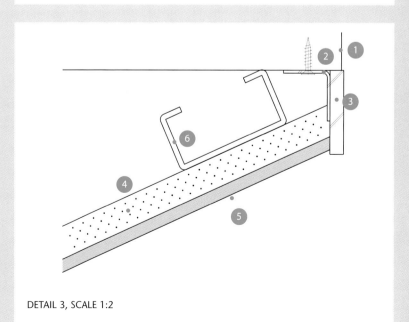

DETAIL 3, SCALE 1:2

DURAS, TOKYO
SINATO

The original 3.65m (12ft)-high ceiling in this shopping mall unit is too low for two separate floor levels and unnecessarily high for a space in which customers' attention should and would be concentrated on merchandise displayed at and below eye level. The potential of the height prompted the idea of introducing a second ceiling plane, of expanded metal sheet, at the more conventional height of 2.25m (7½ft), in which there were two voids, each located over a stepped platform.

The platforms, finished in a cement render on a timber frame to match the floor surface, divide the floor into zones with a 'long' route around them and a 'short' route across the lower steps. Customers may climb to the top of the platforms, over which the mesh ceiling has been omitted, and look across the upper face of the suspended mesh. Each platform is crowned with a baroque black sofa, as a counterpoint to the austerity of all other elements. The lower steps and underside of projecting steps provide horizontal display surfaces and access to garments hung from the mesh ceiling.

The palette of materials throughout the shop is rigorously restrained. Black steel sections (25mm/1in.) act as ceiling grid members, hanging rails and furniture legs. The repetitious use of naked light bulbs, whose flex emerges directly from the plaster of the ceiling, emphasizes the austerity. Apart from the sofas, only the circular 'candelabra' begin to hint at flamboyance, but their geometry and location conform to the inherent logic of the square grid.

The perimeter walls, white to a height of 2.25m (7½ft), are slightly dappled by shadows cast by the ceiling mesh. Above the suspended ceiling they are lined with mirrors, which reflect the hanging light bulbs to infinity. The glass handrails of the platforms add further layers of transparency and reflection for additional blurring of boundaries and planes.

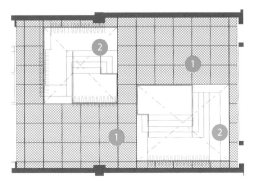

UPPER LEVEL, SCALE 1:200

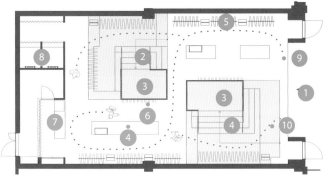

LOWER LEVEL, SCALE 1:200

DURAS

ABOVE
The finish of the stepped platforms matches the concrete floor screed. The black square-sectioned metal tube serves as furniture framing, hanging rails and support grid for the suspended ceiling.

LEFT
Upper level
1 Mesh ceiling
2 Void
Lower level
1 Entrance
2 Steps
3 Platform
4 Plinth display
5 Floor-mounted display rail
6 Display rail suspended below platform
7 Counter
8 Changing rooms
9 Long route around platforms
10 Short route over platforms

RIGHT
Section
1 Polished concrete screed
2 Timber framing for platform
3 See detail on page 89
4 Glass balustrade
5 Concealed hanging rail
6 Suspended mesh ceiling
7 Wall mirror above ceiling
8 Hanging wire
9 Candelabra

SECTION, SCALE 1:50

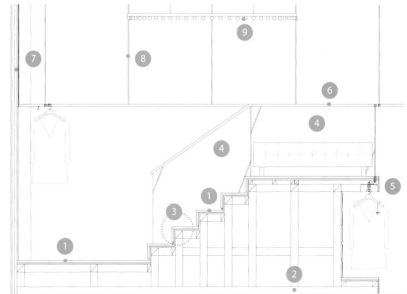

LEFT
The transparency and reflectivity of glass balustrades, high-level mirrors and mesh make boundaries ambiguous.

BELOW LEFT
The mesh acts as a display surface on the upper levels. Mirrors on the walls above the ceiling reflect the lights, and customers, to infinity.

OPPOSITE PAGE, TOP
The display system is also a stair over which the mesh ceiling is omitted to allow access to the raised display.

OPPOSITE PAGE, BOTTOM LEFT
All components are precisely defined but pale shadows cast by mesh make a discreet unifying pattern.

OPPOSITE PAGE, BOTTOM RIGHT
Detail of platform step
1 In situ sand and cement
2 Expanded metal reinforcement
3 Plywood
4 Timber frame
5 Aluminium channel recess

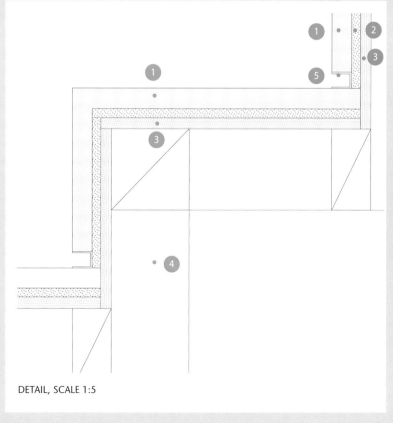

DETAIL, SCALE 1:5

FIFTH AVENUE SHOE REPAIR, STOCKHOLM
GUISE

Fifth Avenue Shoe Repair is a Swedish fashion brand, which 'deconstructs traditional typologies of shoes and clothes and creates new hybrid garments'. This interior, in Stockholm's fashion district, a prototype for future locations, sets out to reflect that principle, most evidently in the mutation of the elements of a stair into the dominant display element. The original double helix form of the plan and section evolved in response to the practical priorities of display and circulation.

While the 'stair' provides the signature element within the store, delicate matrices of steel rods, forming 360 x 360 x 360mm(14⅛in.) cubes, provide secondary, more utilitarian, floor and wall-hung shelving units that can be easily rearranged to meet the particular restrictions of other building shells. Thin black steel plates may be placed within the web of rods to make shelves. The skeleton frame allows front and side hanging for garments.

The cuboid rod structures also provide vertical support for the thin, folded sheet that forms the 'stair' display and 6mm (¼in.) welded steel ribs provide the additional stiffening that maintains the angles between the nominal treads and risers. The upper horizontal plate is secured to, but visually separated from, the ceiling plane.

The visual primacy of the comparatively delicate 'stair' and shelving is emphasized by their blackness against the universal whiteness of other elements. This is also reinforced by the elimination of skirting and trimming around doors to changing cubicles and the greys of the shadows they would generate. The only other black elements, chairs and handrail, share the sparse linearities of the display elements.

RIGHT
The cuboid skeleton, complemented by the linearity of the black chair, supports thin steel plates that carry merchandise and provide rails for front and side hanging.

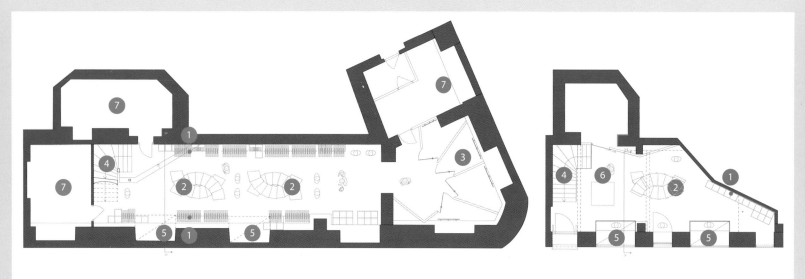

BASEMENT PLAN, SCALE 1:200

GROUND FLOOR PLAN, SCALE 1:200

ABOVE
Basement and ground floor plans
1 'Cube' wall display
2 Stair display
3 Changing rooms
4 Stair
5 Void
6 Counter
7 Store

BELOW
Cubes of visually delicate black steel
rods provide vertical support for the thin
folded plate of the 'stair' display and a
basic structure for the wall-hung shelving.

RIGHT
Top: the 'stair' is formed from a
continuous sheet of 1.2mm (1/20in.)
powder-coated steel.
Middle: the sheet is folded to form
irregularly dimensioned 'treads' and
'risers'.
Bottom: 6mm (1/4in.) steel flats stiffen the
structure. Fixing rods separate the top
tread from the ceiling to eliminate visual
contact.
1 Steps, folded steel 1.2mm sheet
2 Reinforcement, welded steel 6mm flats
3 Support, welded steel 6mm rods

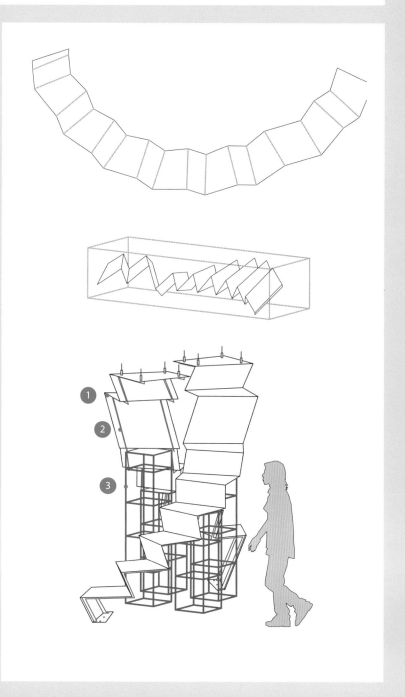

RIGHT
Section through ground and basement floors
The folded display 'stair', aligned on both floors and close to the stair visually links the levels. The cutting back of the ground floor opens up views to the basement.

BELOW LEFT
Steel flats, 6mm (¼in.), welded to the reverse side of the 'treads' and 'risers' stiffen and maintain angles.

BELOW RIGHT
Changing rooms
Skirtings and door trims are eliminated to maintain the planar purity of white surfaces.

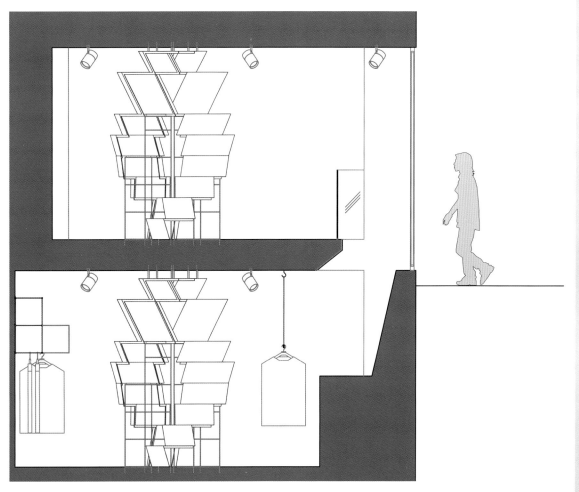

SECTION, SCALE 1:50

H+M, HARAJUKU, TOKYO
UNIVERSAL DESIGN STUDIO

The designers were asked to create an identity for the clothes chain's first flagship stores in Asia, to communicate, directly and dynamically, the brand's commitment to progressive design. They developed prototypes for façades and stairs, elements that would be adaptable to different contexts.

The site for the store in Harajuku provided the opportunity to move away from the chain's normal 'black box' solution, to reject the anonymous façade that excluded light from the interior in favour of allowing natural light and views of the street to become part of the customers' experience.

An outer clear-glass façade provides weatherproofing, and an inner screen of white metal ribs allows light in and views out of the building as well as glimpses of the interior from the street. At street level the perimeter zone, between outer skin and ribs, becomes a display window. Each rib has a mirror-polished steel inset, which ensures that perimeter walls are perpetually transformed, both internally and externally, by changes in light conditions and movement inside and outside the store. Steel struts at top and bottom allow the ribs to float clear of floor and ceiling, as a distinctly separate element in the layering of the façade.

The ribs are also used to transform the stairwell into a separate environment that maintains some links, visual and physical, to the activities of the four sales floors. While the stair is located within a conventional extruded rectangular volume, its plan tapers and inflects at each floor level. The ribs twist as they rise to accommodate the changes and their linearity traces out and makes clear the mutating shape of the enclosure.

TOP RIGHT
The illuminated façades at night illustrate the permeability of the screen walls.

RIGHT
Ribs in the stairwell are connected to a tubular steel structure with the same struts used in the façade screen.

OPPOSITE PAGE
The front elevation by day showing the glazed outer skin and ribbed inner screen that replace the conventional blank walls of the city centre retail store, filtering light and views into and out of the interior.

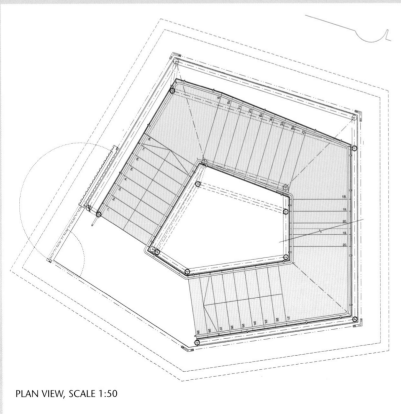

PLAN VIEW, SCALE 1:50

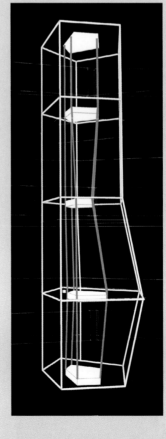

ABOVE
A view looking up showing changes in plan at each floor level.

FAR LEFT
Plan of stairwell
Dotted lines show lines of enclosures above and below.

LEFT
Skeletal view of stairwell. White lines represent the screens to the sales floors and blue those to the central void.

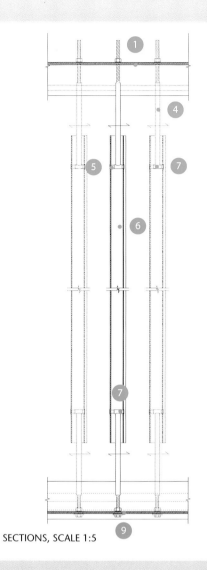
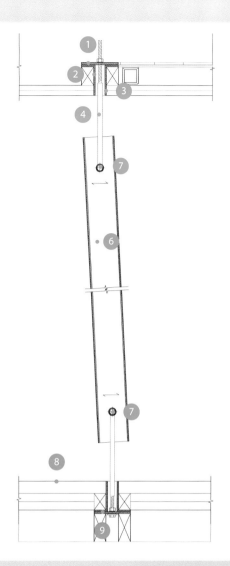
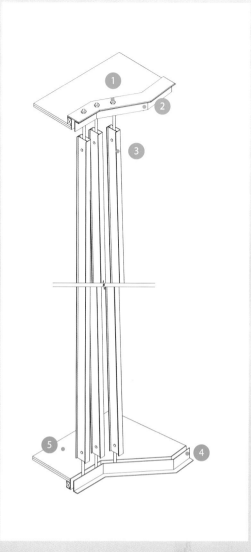

SECTIONS, SCALE 1:5

ABOVE LEFT & MIDDLE
Cross section through slats
1 Steel plate to sit above profile with predrilled holes. Strut connections to fix into plate
2 Track at head and base fabricated from steel sections
3 Plasterboard skimmed to track edge.
4 Steel strut fixed into ceiling plate. Finished white
5 Neoprene washers
6 Aluminium slats
7 Pin joint at head and base. Connection slotted to allow vertical movement
8 Floor finish to run tight to edge of profile track
9 Steel strut fixed into subfloor through profile track

ABOVE RIGHT
Façade fixing sketch
1 Slat strut to sit in track, mechanically fixed at head
2 Track inset flush to ceiling level
3 Aluminium slats set out along façade in modules from main setting out line following profiles to head and base
4 Track at head and base fabricated from steel sections
5 Finished floor level

RIGHT
A model that illustrates how the filtering metal ribs sit behind the outer clear glazed weathering façade, which is supported on the ribs that hang from the projecting floor above.

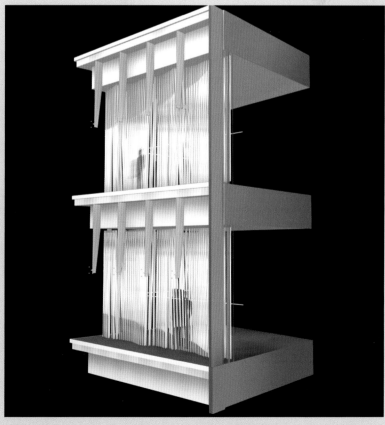

H+M,
LOS ANGELES
UNIVERSAL DESIGN STUDIO

This second solution to the expression of H+M brand values is generated by its location on a long, wide North American shopping strip. The store needs to draw attention to itself, to create an impression on drive-by shoppers, and it is obliged to make a large-scale statement, rather than the more delicate gesture that works for pedestrians on a Japanese city centre street.

The original building shell is long and low and the addition of a continuously changing façade of sharply creased metal panels, when viewed from a passing car, makes a trademark kinetic experience. A pedestrian approaching the building is equally involved by the scale and folded precision of the angular profile overhead. Crucial to the success of both experiences is the location's reliable, strong sunlight, which maximizes the modelling of the façade. The panels project a metre in front of the street-level glazing and define an area of pavement that belongs to the store, implying that the customer has already crossed the threshold.

Even for a large expanse of wall it is expensive to produce variations of prefabricated panel types and heavily modelled façades tend to become repetitive and monotonous if the basic unit, or limited range of units, can be recognized and the repetitious rhythm of their assembly understood. This installation had only two panel types but by staggering the order and rotating them vertically it has been possible to make what reads as a non-repeating linear pattern. At horizontal joints the profiles meet exactly when lower panels are inverted to mirror the upper. A horizontal panel closes the gap between the folded metal and the glazed façades.

TOP RIGHT
The projecting façade creates a pedestrian zone around the glazed area of the façade. Panels do not touch the ground, allowing their lower edge to read cleanly above the less perfect pavement.

RIGHT
The crisp folds of the long, low façade present a kinetic trademark to passing motorists.

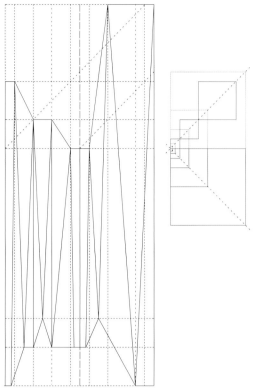

DETAIL

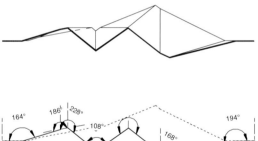

DETAIL

ABOVE
Façade folding details

ABOVE RIGHT
Strong lighting, both natural and artificial, maximizes the three-dimensionality of the panelled façade.

RIGHT
3D model of façade detail.
The new façade projects beyond the original structure on steel framing. An aluminium panel (1) closes the gap between old and new.

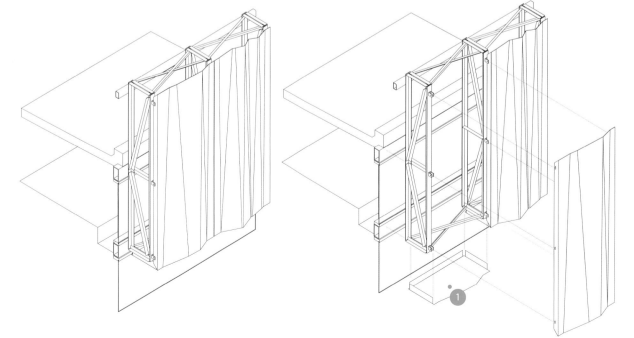

LABELS, SITTARD
MAURICE MENTJENS

The floor area divides naturally into three distinct spaces, the result of the extension of the original shop into the building next door and the enclosure, with a glazed roof, of the former long, narrow garden between them.

Customers enter into the 'garden' space, now lined with steel 'trees', cut out by water jet and powder coated. The floor is bisected by white and black resin strips. The white adjoins and leads into the larger women's area, with its well-lit, predominantly white finishes and fittings. The black leads to the men's zone, with heavier detailing, darker colours and lower light levels. The reveals of the opening to the women's section are painted white and those to the men's black.

Cantilevered sales counters project into the central space to make a three-dimensional connection between the white and black zones. These veneered units, sympathetic in colour to the exposed brickwork of the central area, are supported off the existing walls and, towards the extremity of the cantilever, on a discreet clear acrylic leg.

Vertical and slightly inclined powder-coated steel tubes in the white space support stainless steel hanging rails and clear acrylic circular shelves. Halogen lights, recessed into the ceiling in circles, alternate with circular fluorescent fittings. Circles are repeated in the wall recesses, with steel back plates on which magnetized pins support bags and shoes.

In the black space merchandise is supported on a lattice of wooden beams. On the long wall horizontal beams support clothes racks. On the opposite wall beams carry sweaters, shoes and accessories. Strip lights illuminate clothing on hangers and halogen spotlights provide highlights.

ABOVE
Steel 'trees' sit against the exposed brickwork of the former exterior walls to the garden. The white resin floor in the women's area and black in the men's area, spill out and bisect the floor.

RIGHT
Steel 'tree' forms are cut by water jet and powder coated.

FAR RIGHT
Branches may also act as hanging rails.

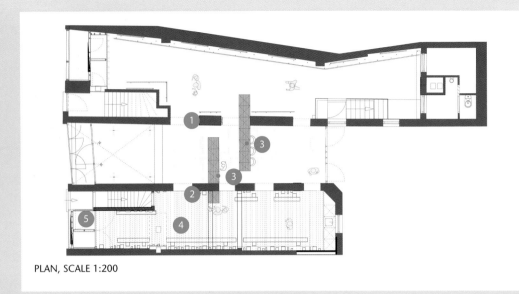

PLAN, SCALE 1:200

LEFT
Plan
1 Womenswear
2 The 'garden' entrance zone
3 Counters
4 Menswear
5 Changing rooms
6 Window display

BELOW
Plan and elevation of counter in menswear section.

OPPOSITE PAGE
Cantilevered counters connect the white and black spaces to the entrance area and each other. The clear acrylic leg support for the cantilever is visible.

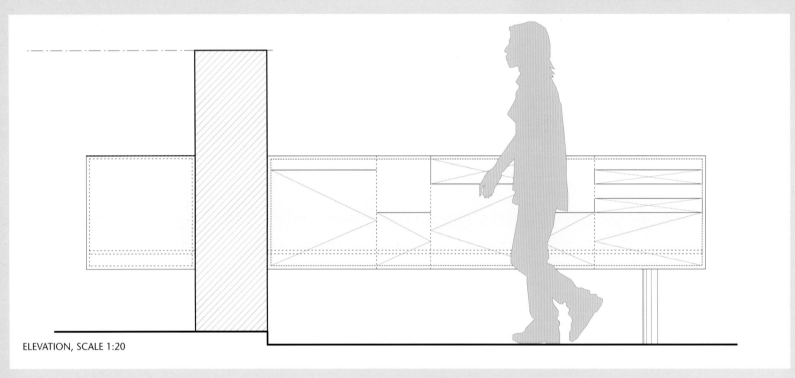

ELEVATION, SCALE 1:20

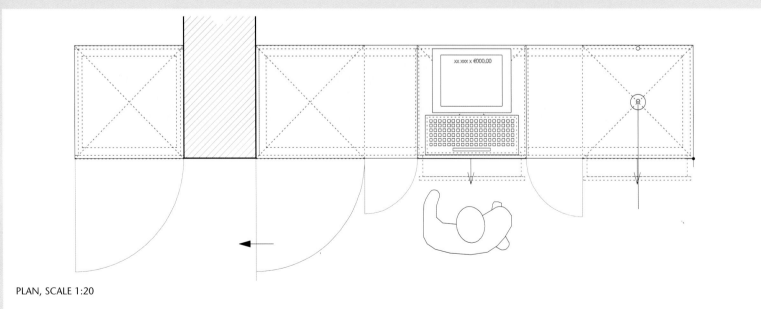

PLAN, SCALE 1:20

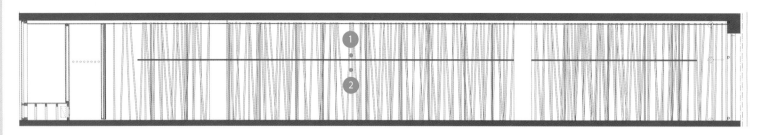

ELEVATION, SCALE 1:100

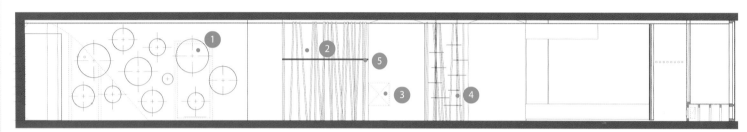

ELEVATION, SCALE 1:100

TOP
Womenswear
The horizontal hanging rail is supported by angled tubes.
1 Hanging rail
2 Angled tubes

ABOVE
Womenswear
1 Wall recesses with steel plates and magnetized pins
2 Inclined white rods
3 Counter
4 Round acrylic tables on white rods
5 Hanging rail

BELOW LEFT
White powder-coated steel tubes that support hanging rails and acrylic shelves provide visual texture within the white space. Those leaning forward make room for the garments to hang clear of the walls.

BELOW RIGHT
Circular recesses with steel back plates and magnetized pins repeat the geometry of recessed ceiling lights.

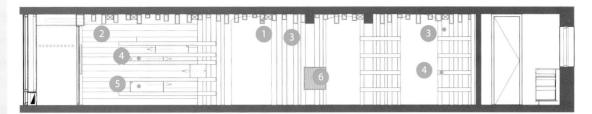

ELEVATION, SCALE 1:100

ABOVE
Menswear
1 Dark-stained timber 'beams'
2 Dark-stained horizontal timber wall cladding
3 Dark-stained timber vertical 'posts'
4 Dark-stained timber shelves
5 Glass display cabinet
6 Counter

BELOW
Menswear
Dark-stained timber surfaces of the smaller men's zone contrast with more delicate white elements in the women's area.

LURDES BERGADA, BARCELONA
DEARDESIGN

The client is an established Spanish fashion company, known for simple, well-made, functional clothing.

The shop is divided into two distinct areas. One, devoted to the sparse display of clothes in a stark space, is an accomplished reinterpretation of a well-tested formula. The other, a cocoon that contains the practical supporting spaces, changing rooms, storage and services within a complex wooden structure, is assembled from 1,000 pieces of pre-cut plywood, screwed to a skeleton of horizontal and vertical plywood ribs.

The finishes and elements of the display area relate as much, perhaps more, to the landscape beyond the glazed entrance wall than they do to the complex geometry of the plywood skin. Planar simplicity is underlined by the massive rectangle of a solid wooden bench and the minimal metal hanging rails. The solidity of cement-rendered walls and concrete floor contrast with the lightness and fragility of the beech veneers of the faceted plywood construction.

The plywood installation was built on site from irregular triangles, each unique, defined and dimensioned by computer, and numbered to ease the assembly process. When inside it customers can see and understand the 'secrets' of its intricate construction, as they would the making of a garment if they were to deconstruct it. Screws, the designers say, represent stitching, and the pencilled numbers are equivalent to the chalk marks made by a pattern cutter.

The charm of the design is that this most complex, digitally generated object ultimately relies on familiar materials and easily comprehensible manual techniques for its realization.

RIGHT
The lightweight and intricate plywood structure sits alongside the raw finishes and more elemental forms of the display area.

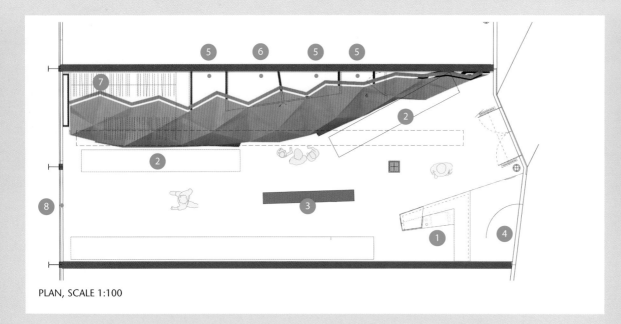

PLAN, SCALE 1:100

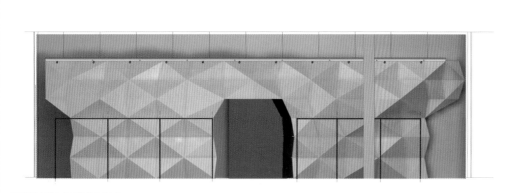

ELEVATION, SCALE 1:100

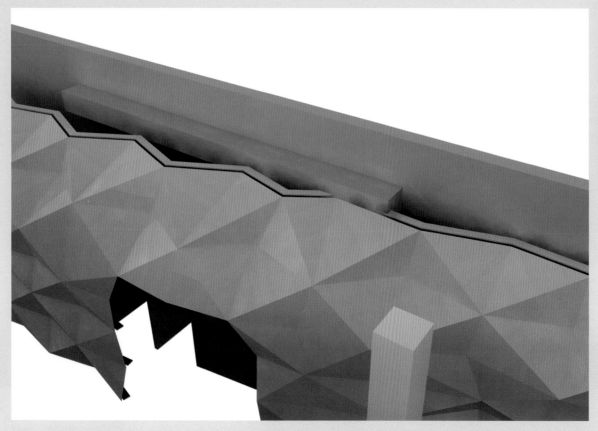

ABOVE
The external perfection of the cocoon belies the complexity of the assembly process, which is reflected and revealed in the changing area mirror.

RIGHT
The precision of the plywood construction contrasts with the rawness of other elements.

ABOVE
Fixing mechanisms and pencilled panel numbers make the assembly process wholly comprehensible.

LEFT
Horizontal and vertical plywood ribs make the skeleton that shapes the external skins.

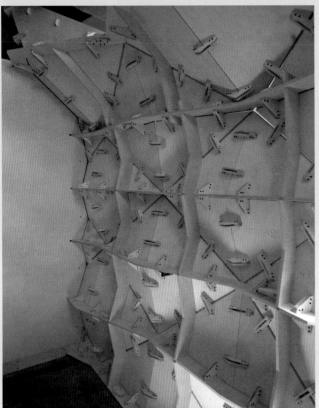

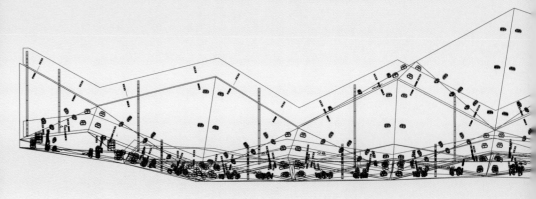

RIGHT
From within, the delicacy of the structure is clear, and it appears more fragile against the solidity of the sales area.

BELOW
The cutting of components and the complexity of their construction was made possible by CNC techniques.

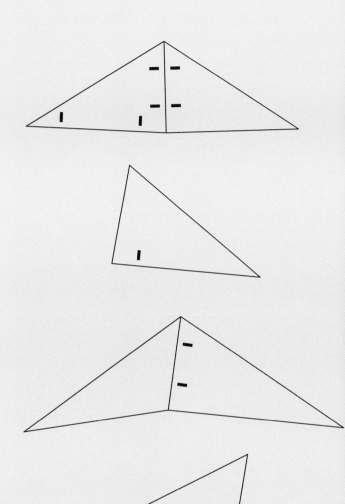

NOTE,
OITA
CASE-REAL

Commitment to reflecting brand values has here resulted in what might appear to be an extravagantly radical approach to this conversion of a small, 60sq m (646sq ft) unit in the Japanese coastal city of Oita. The existing glazed façade followed the line of a pedestrian passageway rather than the geometry of the other three walls and was subdivided asymmetrically by structural walls. It was deemed to present too great a compromise in the making of views to a sparse and purist interior.

The solution was to remove the original windows, strip back the opening and create a single pristine window behind to give an uninterrupted view to the new interior. The found textures and colours exposed in cutting through the existing construction were left unfinished and exposed, in extreme contrast to the perfection of the new glazed opening, which is framed by the black-dyed ash veneer of the fascia and door, on which the only visible ironmongery is the lock at pavement level. The black-dyed ash is reiterated in the low block that carries the window display and which sits on the white painted floorboards.

The wedge of floor between the old and the new façade lines establishes a degree of compatibility between the two. Polished pebbles reflect both the rawness of the exposed construction and the black gloss of the new façade. White urethane painted boards connect the new door to the existing passageway, a bridge that emphasizes the disconnection between new and old.

The new interior is strictly rectilinear. Untidy services and storage are tucked into the space behind the public stair

TOP
The purist interior contrasts with the messiness of the world beyond the buffer zone created between the new and old façades.

RIGHT
At night the illuminated interior glows in the dark buffer zone between it and the original façade.

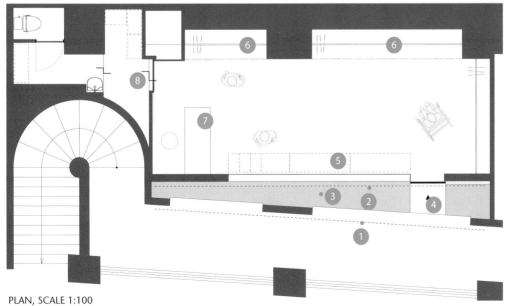

PLAN, SCALE 1:100

ABOVE
The wall of the old façade is cut open and no attempt is made to cosmeticize the edges of the new openings. The new, refined, façade is set back on its own geometry.

LEFT
Plan
1 Original façade line
2 New façade
3 Pebbles
4 Wooden bridge
5 Window display
6 Hanging rails
7 Counter
8 Services

OILILY, ANTWERP
UXUS

The found object may be treated reverently, sentimentally or ironically, depending on its perceived aesthetic merit or provenance. Normally its value depends on its being intact. This project is interesting because it takes a collection of undistinguished pieces of domestic furniture and amends them with what, at first glance, appears to be a clumsy disregard of their original structure but which, on closer examination, is a well-considered and deliberate and witty intention to conjoin them with basic and bland elements of conventional retail display furniture.

The designers' intention is clearly signalled by the position of the cuts made in the existing pieces. Lines of mouldings and panelling are disregarded and the dimensions that determine the location of cuts are governed by the practicalities and priorities of display. No attempt is made to reconcile the aesthetic of the new with the old. Colours and whimsy prevail, in sympathy with the merchandise but at odds with the solemn brown-stained timbers of the pieces they transform.

The one wholly new element, the conical structure in the atrium, retains the directness of construction that is characteristic of the composite pieces. The practical logic of the metal joint connectors and the pulley system that raises and lowers the hanging figures is transparent.

Behind the glazed screens around the void are showrooms for trade sales and, while superficially more serious, the domesticity of tables and chairs, the prevailing ivory-white colour and the ad hoc quality of the curtain room dividers present a more adult, but persistently whimsical, aesthetic. Glimpses of mannequins suspended in the atrium present the only colour on the upper level.

TOP
Chairs are crudely painted, stacked and screwed together to form an ostensibly precarious display system. Backs of chairs on the lower levels are sawn off for better vertical alignment.

BOTTOM
A sawn-off door gives access to the remaining shell of a wardrobe converted into a child-scaled room.

OPPOSITE PAGE, TOP LEFT
A chair with curved plan and rounded detail is inserted, with sawn-off legs, into the strictly square-edged display unit. Right-angled steps allow children to climb into the chair for fittings.

OPPOSITE PAGE, TOP RIGHT
A timber structure rises through two floors of the atrium. Timber connectors and pulleys to hoist the mannequins into place are clearly visible.

OPPOSITE PAGE, BOTTOM LEFT
The upper section of a wardrobe, sawn off without regard for the pattern of original mouldings and panelling, is perched on top of a mundane square-sectioned metal hanging rail.

OPPOSITE PAGE, BOTTOM RIGHT
The predominantly ivory-white trade sales area on the upper level presents a more conventionally elegant place to do business without wholly abandoning quirky gestures.

3.1 PHILLIP LIM, SEOUL
LEONG LEONG

This project is one in a series created by the designers for the Lim brand. Each interior offers variations on shared themes, that the designers describe as 'No Joints, Just Fields...', in which rather than emphasizing joints between surfaces their strategy is 'to accentuate each surface as a continuous field of texture and material'.

The new 20m (66ft)-high façade wraps the existing building shell in a continuous skin of eight different 600 x 600mm (23⅝ x 23⅝in.) panel types that flatten progressively towards the top of the building and eliminate indications of different floor levels. Door and window openings do not coincide with panel joints and cut through the façade as if at odds with its pattern.

Curved walls subdivide the plan on both floors, creating intimate sales areas and changing rooms and concealing stores and services. Interior walls have different visual textures that refer to materials used in the brand's other stores. (Acoustic foam pyramids used in the Los Angeles store here transmute into cones.) The designers worked directly with a specialist manufacturer to develop five foam panel types that could be assembled so that the density of cones reduced towards the perimeters of walls, suggesting that the texture pattern was particular to each wall.

Continuous and evolving patterns appear on floors, in which materials modulate through several tones of grey from the entrance to the rear of the shop and walls, where the implied perspective of various sizes of wallpaper motifs suggests that they are floating off into an infinite space. Physical boundaries are eroded by mirrors on perimeter walls, which complete the circles implied by the curved walls and extend planes of texture and pattern.

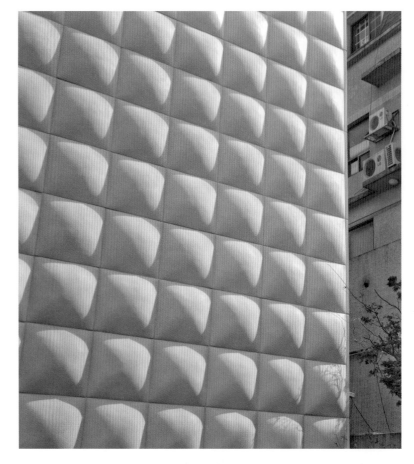

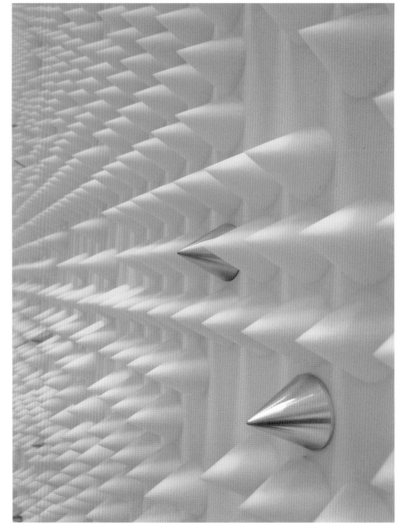

TOP
New external cladding eliminates evidence of existing floor levels.

RIGHT
The aggregation of cones on the internal wall panels repeats the obsessive repetition of the external cladding panels. The distribution of brass cones mimics the seemingly random insertion of windows on the exterior.

OPPOSITE PAGE
Openings in the façade do not relate to the panel grid, giving them more visually complex edge conditions.

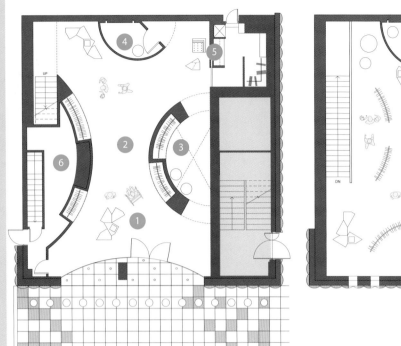

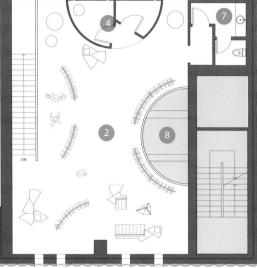

LEFT
Ground and upper floor plan
1 Entrance
2 Main retail area
3 Secondary retail area
4 Changing rooms
5 Point of sale
6 Storage
7 Washroom
8 Void

BELOW
View from the entrance. The smaller,
double-height retail area is to the right.

GROUND FLOOR PLAN, SCALE 1:200   UPPER FLOOR PLAN, SCALE 1:200

RIGHT
Mirrors extend the spaces, completing
the circles begun by semicircular walls
and doubling the impact of two and
three-dimensional patterns.

MIDDLE
An internal wall panel.

BELOW
The tones of marble and timber floor
have affinity with the shadows of the
panelled walls. The handrail matches the
brass cones.

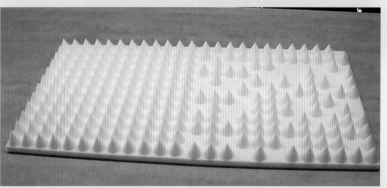

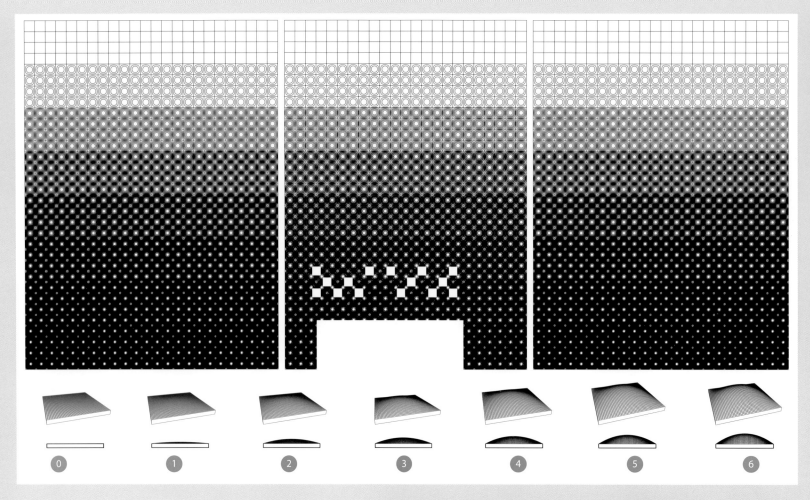

LEFT
The free-standing building is wholly
reclad in a skin of modelled panels.

ABOVE & BELOW
Cladding panels
The façade is clad in seven different panel
types, most bulbous on the bottom
graded through to flat on top.
1. Type 00
2. Type 01
3. Type 02
4. Type 03
5. Type 04
6. Type 05
7. Type 06

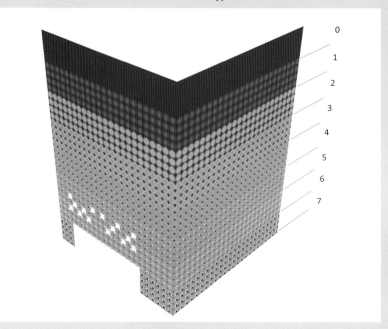

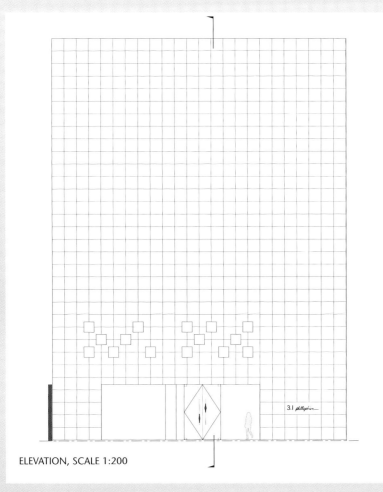

ELEVATION, SCALE 1:200

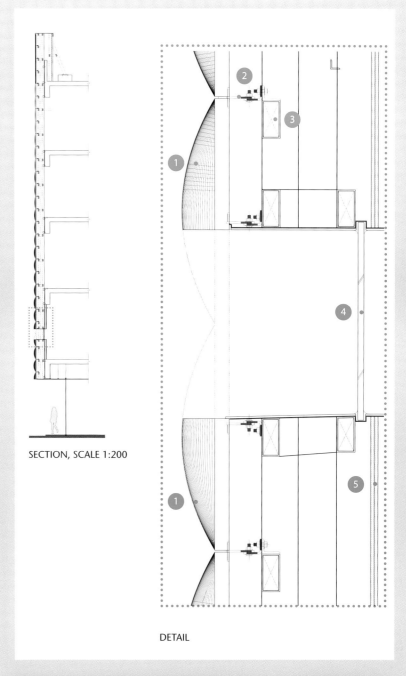

SECTION, SCALE 1:200

DETAIL

ABOVE
The grid of the panels is ignored by the windows, which also do not sit exactly over the entrance slot.

TOP RIGHT
Section through windows
1 'Closed cut' panel around window openings
2 Steel fixing lug screwed to panel and timber framing
3 Timber framing
4 Glass
5 Plasterboard inner skin

RIGHT
Type 01 – one of the eight exterior cladding panel variations.

PLEATS PLEASE, TOKYO
TOKUJIN YOSHIOKA

At first glance this interior appears to conform strictly to minimalist principles: white walls and floor, a few garments on a few simple rails, a rectangular block of a counter, with a green and white suggestion of a cornice as the only visual indulgence.

The columns and beams of the original concrete shell are visible but it becomes clear that they are not the unadorned structural elements they first appear to be; they are uniformly clad in a fine metal mesh. This familiar packaging material, applied obsessively in this unfamiliar context, becomes the defining feature of the interior and the designers' understanding of its practical capacity generates the interior's distinctive aesthetic.

The comparatively pliable mesh can be worked, with a slight radius, easily around simple right-angled horizontal and vertical arrises. At more complex three-dimensional intersections of columns and beams, details for shaping junction pieces have been evolved that deal directly with the problems set by geometry and fabrication, establishing a detailing language unique to the project.

Installation was simple. The mesh is attached with standard cross-head screws to wooden battens that are fixed around columns and beams. Padding behind the mesh eliminates creasing and concave and convex bulging, and ensures smooth rounding at corners.

New smooth white walls, which provide counterpoints to the texture of the mesh, are washed with light to provide the backdrops against which the clothes are hung. Behind them, the rough plaster daubed with green paint provides the only suggestion of the organic.

RIGHT
From the street the mesh cladding of beams and columns is self-effacing, close in colour to the concrete floor and exterior materials.

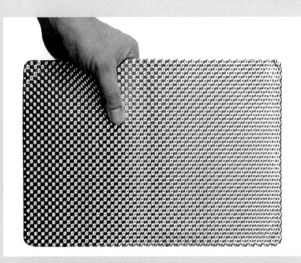

LEFT
The metal mesh cladding.

MIDDLE
The mesh is easy to shape and
holds form well.

BOTTOM
The mesh cladding emerges from
the background and becomes the
defining element of the interior.

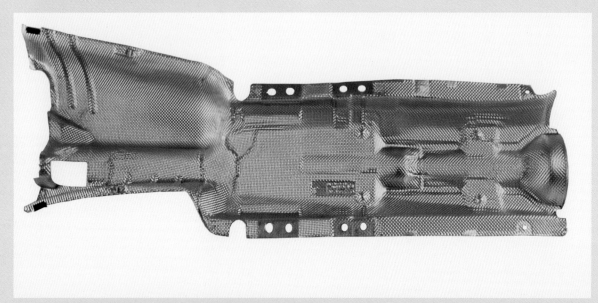

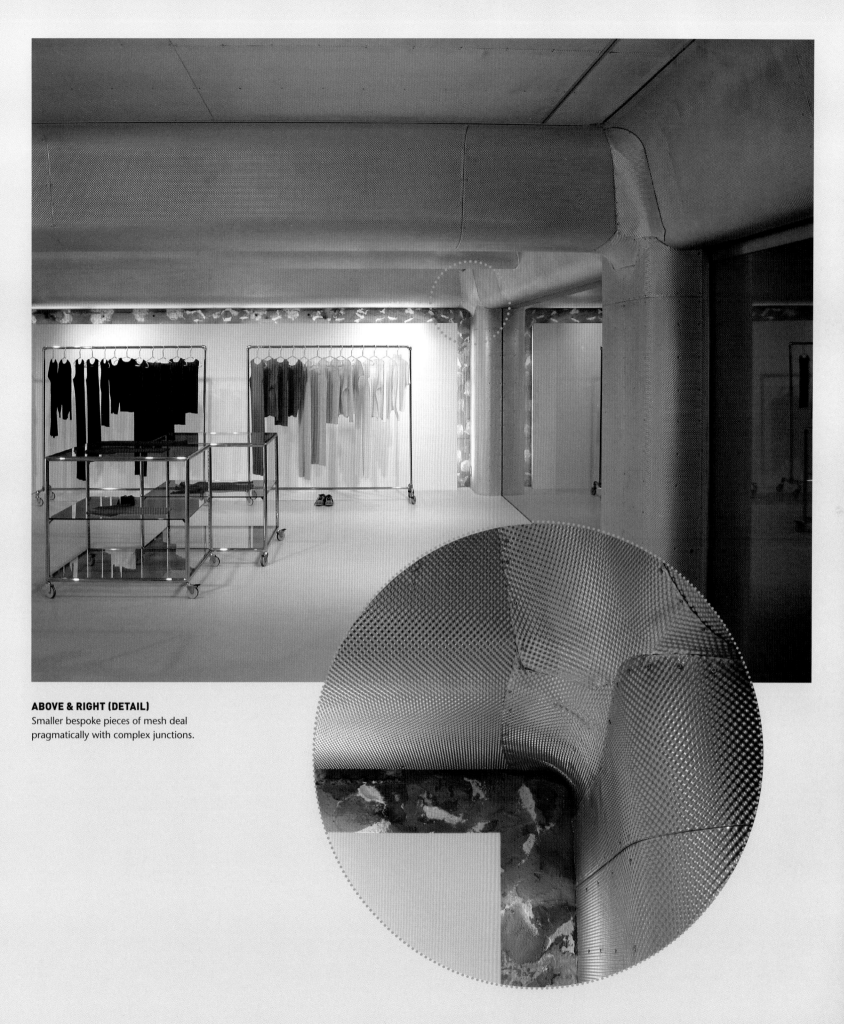

ABOVE & RIGHT (DETAIL)
Smaller bespoke pieces of mesh deal
pragmatically with complex junctions.

POWER PLANT,
TOKYO
GENETO

The concept of 'guerrilla' or 'pop-up' stores – premises rented for a short time and converted into temporary shops – is a familiar one. Diesel Denim Gallery shops in Tokyo and New York build on this idea and invite designers to make temporary installations that are attractions in their own right and also serve to display and sell the brand's more familiar products.

Power Plant succeeds in making a dramatic, diagrammatic gesture, realized with a purity of form that is the result of intelligent and ingenious detail thinking. Its success depends to a great extent on how the angles of the zigzag elements are uncompromised when they meet floor and ceiling, because the means of adding stability to the structure are discreetly downplayed. Ceiling fixings, essential to eliminate movement and vibration, are dimly lit in comparison to the highlights, which are close to them and hold the observer's attention. The apparent slicing of the zigzag into a black display plinth anchors the lower structure at or near its midpoint.

The materials and fixings from which the whole is constructed are happily acknowledged. It is made up of 88 pieces of plywood, some of which were pressure bonded off site to reduce the total to be assembled on site to 28. Each is composed of two layers of 6mm (¼in.) plywood, the ends of which are staggered to provide an overlap for on-site fixing.

The grain of the plywood is allowed to show through the paint and no attempt is made to conceal screws. The designers consider that acknowledgement of material and fixing techniques are appropriate to the brand's values.

RIGHT
The dynamic of the zigzags as they move through the space is consolidated by the lightness with which they touch floor and ceiling and the violence with which they slice into the display plinths.

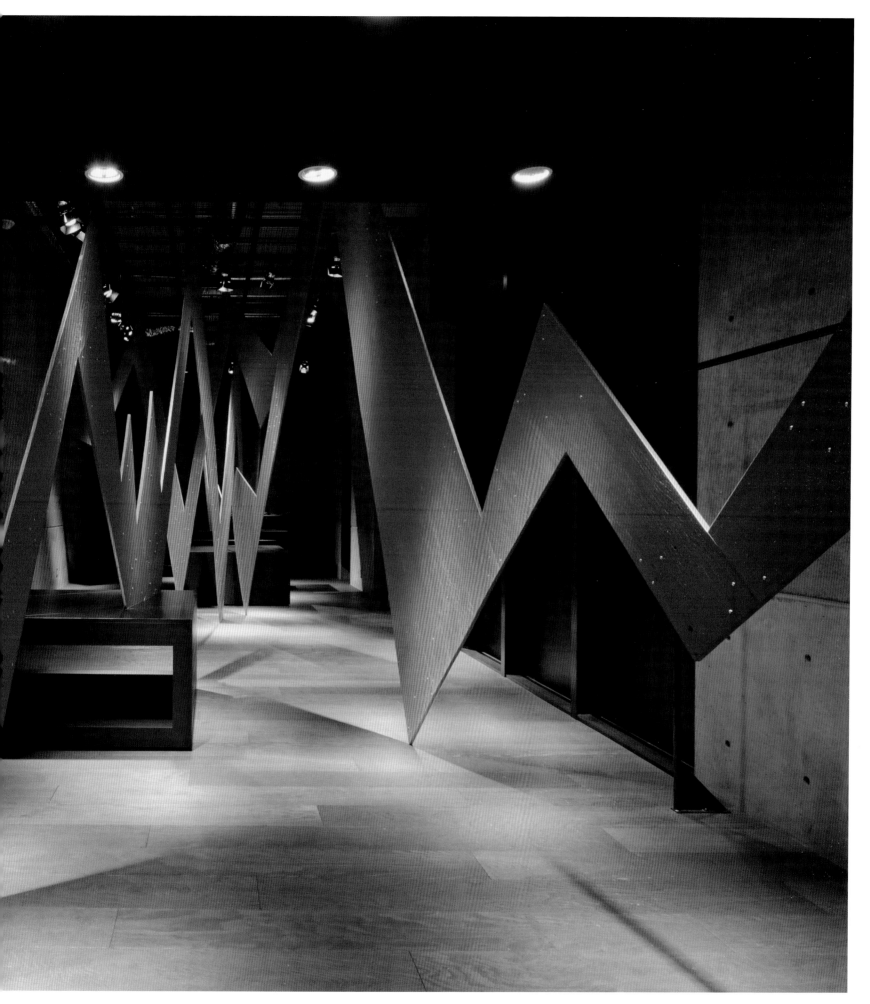

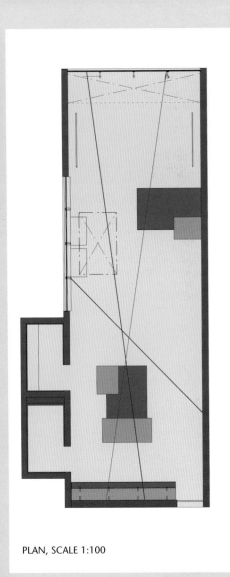

PLAN, SCALE 1:100

LEFT
Plan showing zigzag elements in red

BOTTOM LEFT
Elevations of the individual zigzag elements that criss-cross the gallery indicating the individual components in each.

BELOW & OPPOSITE PAGE
Pressure-bonding techniques were used to assemble 28 components off site. Each comprises two thicknesses of plywood with single thickness projection at each end to provide overlaps that allow strong connections with adjoining components.

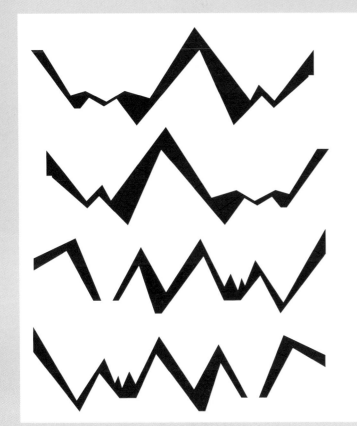

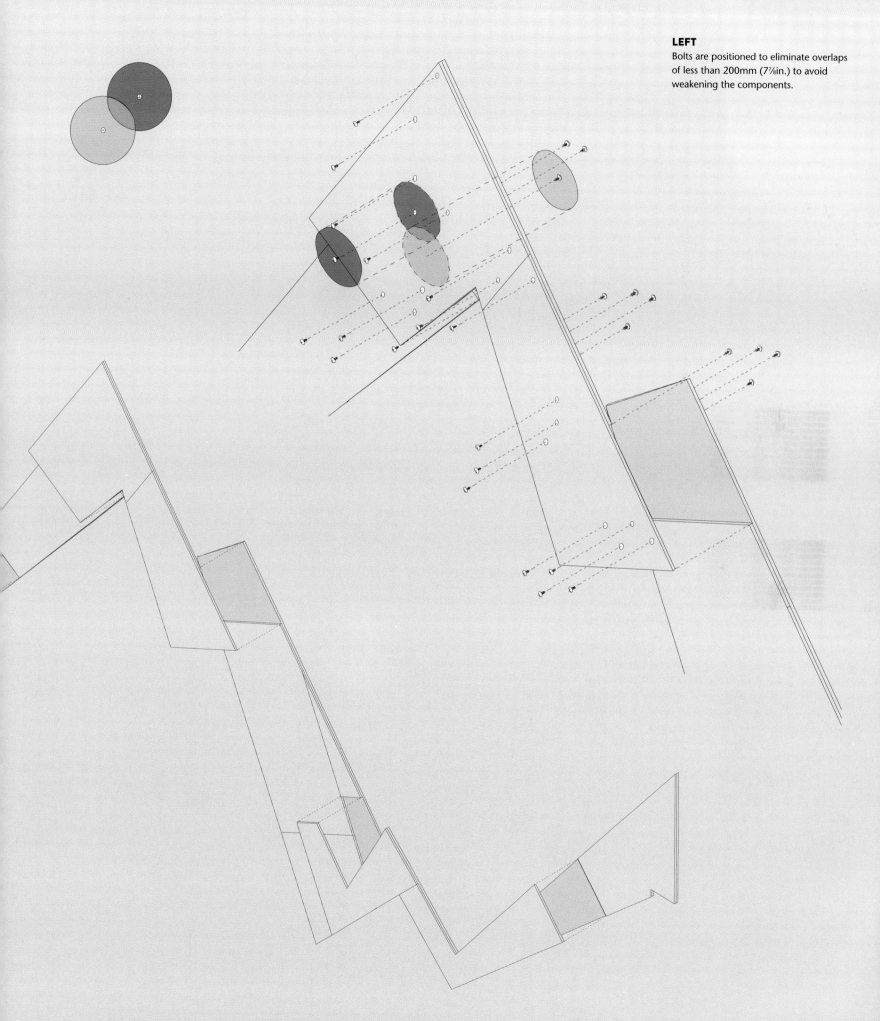

LEFT
The grain of the plywood, the screw heads and the joints in the structure are all exposed.

BELOW
Fixing details
1 Structural ceiling grid
2 1mm (½2in.)-diameter wire
3 Wooden plug
4 Metal sleeve
5 Epoxy acrylic resin adhesive
6 Steel channel
7 Steel bolt

DETAIL, SCALE 1:2

RIGHT
Tubular hanging rails are suspended from the ceiling grid.

BELOW
The low light levels where upper angles meet the ceiling obscure the already minimal fixings. Friction is enough to hold the base angles in position at floor level.

PRECINCT 5, AMSTERDAM
KUUB

The project occupies the top two floors and the street-level entrance lobby of a former police station in Amsterdam. For it the designers created Kube, a modular system of square-section tubular steel, which they used to assemble all new structural and non-structural elements. A Kube assemblage in the entrance lobby signals things to come on the upper levels.

Where function demands it, the framing matrix is infilled with a variety of sheet materials that serve as shelving, screening and stiffening plates, contributing to the rigidity of the whole. To minimize waste, modules relate to standard sheet sizes used in the building industry. Components are comparatively unrefined, drawing on the credibility conferred by utilitarian directness, but are capable of a significant load-bearing capacity.

While there are intriguing modular objects distributed over the generous floor area, the quintessential manifestation of the system is perhaps the structure that dominates the principle double-height space. Parallel long, low display plinths sit on the polished concrete screed floor, directly under tall storage racks that are suspended from refurbished roof trusses. A wheeled ladder, also constructed from Kube components, is pushed along the central slot to give access to high-level storage.

The most impressive structural application of the system is the stair to the mezzanine, which is suspended from the floor plate above and ends one riser's height above the lower floor. The tensile stresses inherent in this configuration challenge both tubular components and joint fixings. Toughened glass between the vertical elements contributes to the rigidity of the whole.

The most expressive use of the system is in the illuminated, partly glazed structure that rears up through the double-height space and over on to the mezzanine, on which a rectangle of framing wrapped in red ribbon calls attention to the upper level.

RIGHT
A Kube assemblage in the street level lobby identifies the shop and anticipates the more complex structures on the upper floors.

ABOVE

The framing system offers dedicated
display places for individual products and
complex long views.

RIGHT

Section
1 Display units
2 Suspended storage racks
3 Kube suspended stair

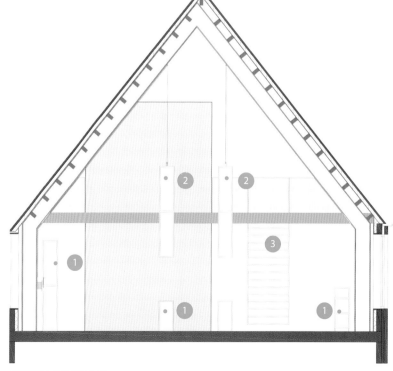

SECTION, SCALE 1:100

RIGHT
Plans

Street level
1 Kube structure
2 Stair
3 Lift

First floor
1 Display units
2 Wheeled ladder
3 Changing rooms
4 Counter
5 Kube stair to mezzanine
6 Lift

Mezzanine
1 Stair
2 Office and staff
3 Suspended storage rack

OPPOSITE PAGE
A wheeled ladder gives access to
high-level storage. The raised
changing cubicle, top left corner,
has mirrored sides.

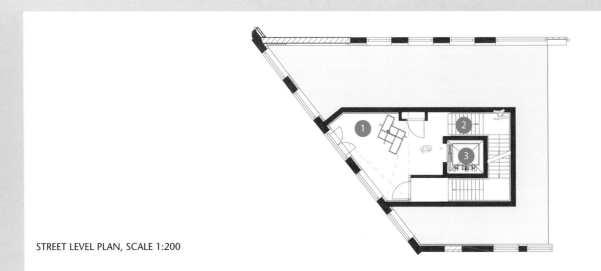

STREET LEVEL PLAN, SCALE 1:200

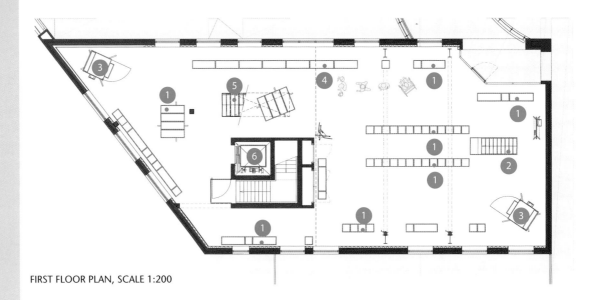

FIRST FLOOR PLAN, SCALE 1:200

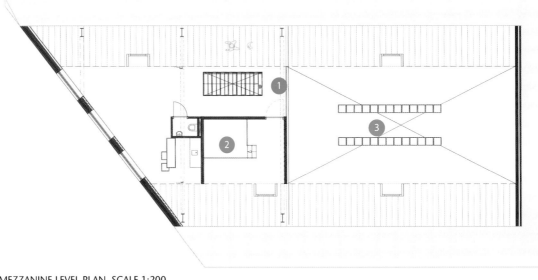

MEZZANINE LEVEL PLAN, SCALE 1:200

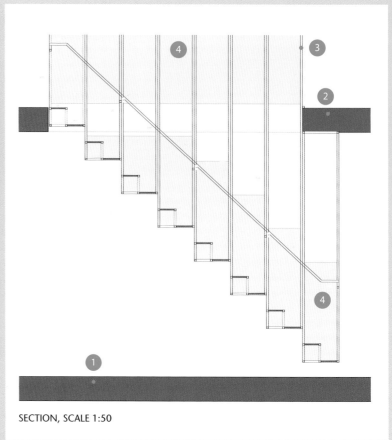

SECTION, SCALE 1:50

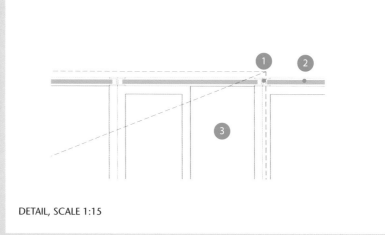

DETAIL, SCALE 1:15

ABOVE

The Kube framed stair, suspended from the concrete floor of the mezzanine stops one riser's height above the lower floor. The counter is on the left.

TOP RIGHT

Section through suspended stair
1 Lower floor slab
2 Mezzanine floor slab
3 Kube tube
4 Glass infill

ABOVE RIGHT

Detail plan of suspended stair
1 Kube tube
2 Glass infill
3 Glass tread

OPPOSITE PAGE

A visually complex structure incorporating lighting, glass and acrylic panels and wrapped framing links the two upper levels.

ROMANTICISM 2, HANGZHOU
SAKO ARCHITECTS

This installation demonstrates how plentiful, cheap, but skilled, labour allows the realization of extraordinarily complex ideas. The boutique, one of a 500-strong chain, is located close to Xihu (West Lake) and the centre of Hangzhou, one of the rapidly developing cities of China.

The designers suggest that the walls, floor and ceiling that enclose an interior protect it as garments protect the body, and draw inspiration from this analogy. What they describe as a 'net' element suggests the fluidity and movement of clothing fabric, while fulfilling the practical obligations of partitioning and furniture. They talk of the net as a third skin, made up of 'bone', which is reinforcing steel rod welded to create the basic armature; 'flesh', which is insulation foam and fibreglass moulded to soften the profiles of struts and junctions; and 'skin', which is a finishing coat of epoxy resin and oil-based paint.

The net structure travels throughout the two levels of the shop, transmuting into a handrail at the stair and free-standing furniture. Indentations in solid vertical surfaces are used to display accessories, to echo the pattern of the net and to help integrate solid and perforated surfaces. Bulbous, solid floor units echo the form of the skeleton structures above them.

The designers have finished the ceiling of the ground floor with polished sheets of stainless steel that increase the apparent height of the room, reflecting and maximizing the complexity of the net structure. They say that the distortion suggests an image reflected in water.

RIGHT
The ubiquitous 'net' structure is reminiscent of the lattice work in traditional Chinese interiors and is reflected in the stainless steel ceiling panels. The solid table mimics the form of the 'net' above.

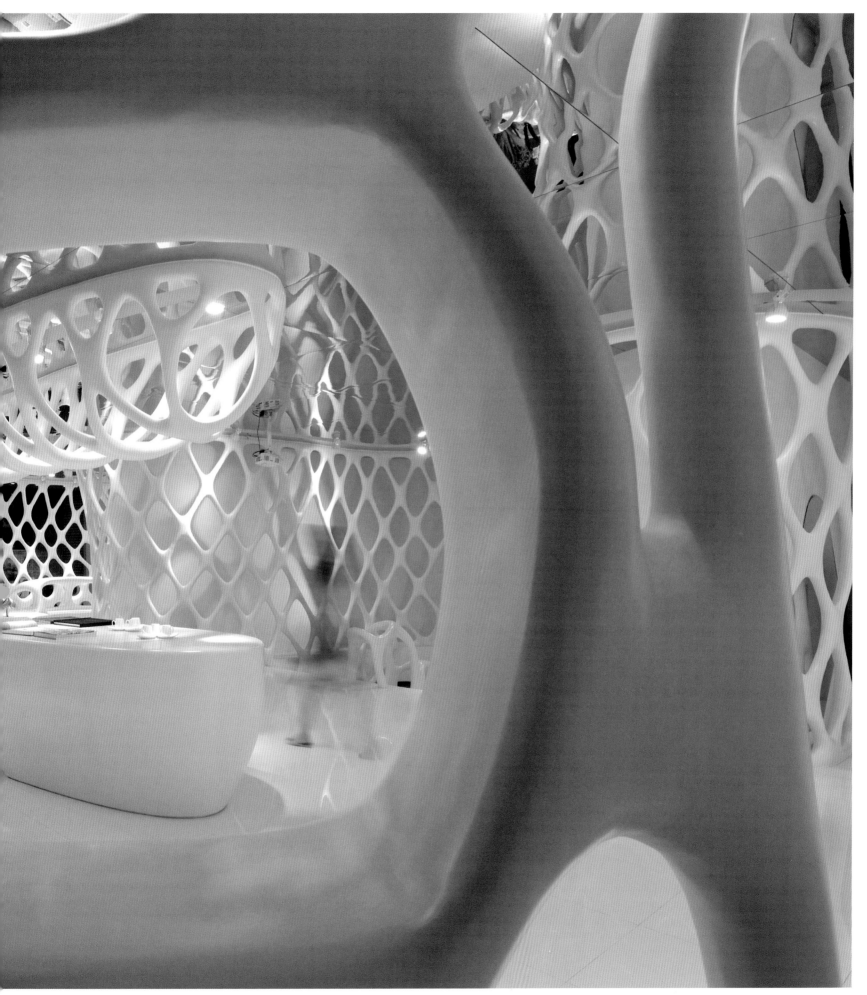

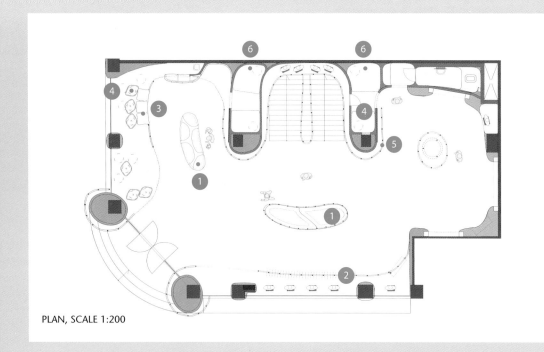

PLAN, SCALE 1:200

LEFT
Plan
1 Display tables
2 The 'net' is cut back to accommodate a hanging rail and views from the street into the shop
3 The 'net' defining the window display space is cut back to accommodate customer seating
4 Customer seating
5 A 'net' screen in front of solid walls masks service areas
6 Changing room

BELOW
The complexity of the grid allows a variety of openings to be made without undermining its inherent rigidity.

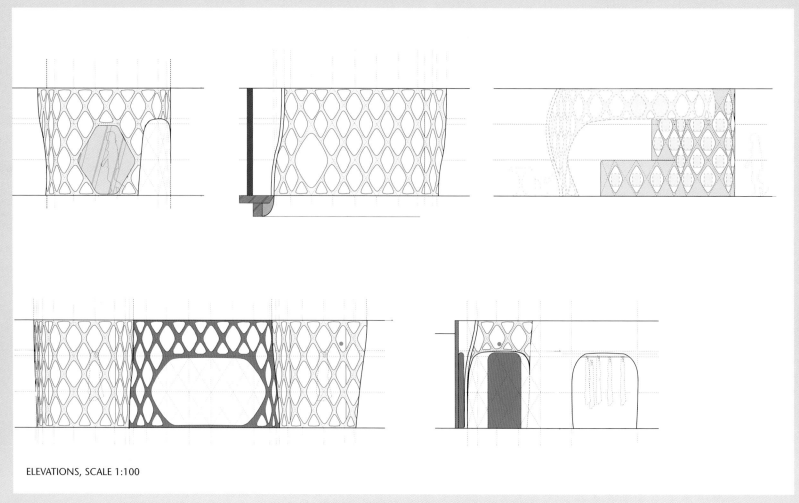

ELEVATIONS, SCALE 1:100

RIGHT
The grid also allows the insertion of less geometrically formal openings with minor variations in thickness.

BELOW
The fluid lines of the 'net' are continued in the junction of solid table components.

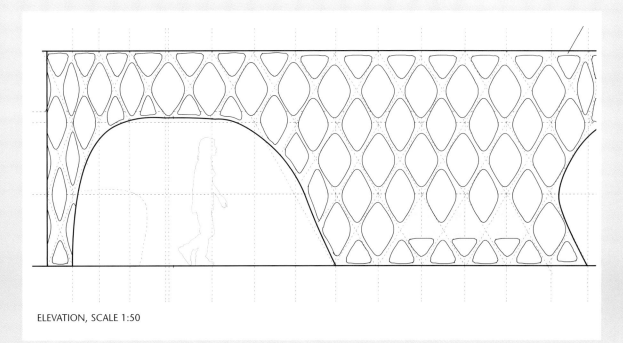

ELEVATION, SCALE 1:50

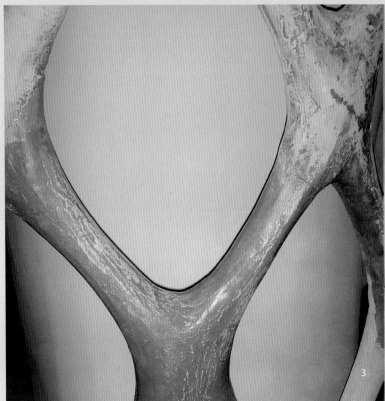

ELEVATION, SCALE 1:10

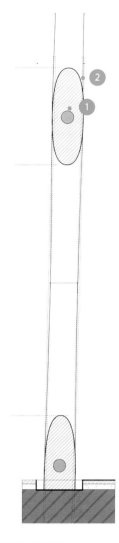

SECTION, SCALE 1:10

OPPOSITE PAGE
Production phases
1 An armature of thin reinforcing steel rods is welded together, on site.
2 This is shaped, and stiffened with insulation foam, applied by hand. It thickens at the junction of the rods to strengthen and ease the junction visually. The thicker, softer visual transition is also easier to finish than an acute angle.
3 The form is refined further with an epoxy resin skin, sanded to give a smoother and regular finished form.
4 Epoxy resin, applied by hand, and water-based paint gives final coherence to the whole.

ABOVE
Elevation and section through 'net'
1 Welded steel reinforcing rods
2 Hand-moulded foam/epoxy resin skin/ paint

RIGHT
The 'net' flows smoothly through three dimensions.

ROLLS, TOKYO
SINATO

This second installation for Diesel Denim Gallery is defined by the performance characteristics of the long, coiled strips of thin aluminium used in its construction; a material as thin as paper but with the strength of metal. Its natural behaviour determines the final form of the elements.

Just as suspended fabrics will find a naturally elegant curve when hung loosely, so the unrolled lengths of aluminium find their own optimum form, but it is one that may be further fine-tuned by the designer, who can determine the sweep of the curve by adjusting the length of strip that is unrolled.

The construction principle is simple, and rewardingly obvious to visitors to the shop/gallery. Rolls of aluminium strip are set on end across the floor and uncoiled enough to allow them to hang loosely from the existing ceiling grid. When two lengths meet at ceiling level they are connected to make a continuous ribbon.

The languid, sweeping curves are not obviously sympathetic to the rectilinear geometry of the existing shell but the natural grey finish of the aluminium sits comfortably against the light grey concrete walls and effectively exploits the existing ceiling lights. The vertical lengths make backdrops for the merchandise on display and subdivide the gallery into more intimate spaces.

The upper surfaces of the rolled drums sitting on the floor act as plinths, and a circle of glass on top makes a smooth display surface. Tight coils in the centre of rolls are pushed upwards to make a second higher plinth, with a spiral of the uncoiling rolls traced on its edges.

TOP
The uncoiling rolls of aluminium catch and reflect artificial lighting.

RIGHT
Plan
1 Coiled drum
2 Suspended uncoiled ribbon
3 Interwinding at ceiling grid support
4 Hanging rails

OPPOSITE PAGE, TOP
Vertical ribbons subdivide the space. Glass discs set on the tightly coiled drums provide an even display surface.

OPPOSITE PAGE, BOTTOM LEFT
The vertical sweep provides a backdrop for displayed products.

OPPOSITE PAGE, BOTTOM RIGHT
Central coils may be pushed up to provide higher plinths.

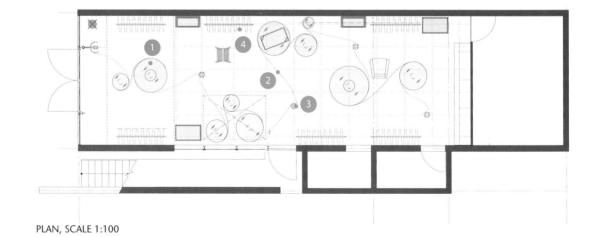

PLAN, SCALE 1:100

STELLA McCARTNEY,
MILAN
APA

For good and obvious reasons, the interiors of fashion shops tend to keep a low profile, deferring to the products. The essential hanging rails tend to be reticent, cantilevered minimally from walls or rising discreetly from the floor. In this interior the dominant elements are the attention-seeking hanging rails.

The conventional working rails that support hangers are masked by fascia components, which provide the aesthetic signature of the interior and visually tidy away the untidy hooks of the hangers. A decorative intention is clear since only part, sometimes none, of the length of each fascia conceals hangers. The supporting rails are straight on plan and curved on elevation, to provide variations appropriate to hanging different garments, but the fascias soar beyond easy reach to decorate the upper walls and swoop down to mark product groupings. A lateral crease gives them rigidity and sharpens the contrast of light and shade.

The working rails are 20mm (¾in.)-diameter steel tubes supported on spigot fixings and offset 300mm (11¾in.) from the face of the wall. Fixings are concealed behind new plasterboard wall linings that project 80mm (3⅛in.) from the face of the existing wall and accommodate edge lighting. A second spigot fixing supports the thin steel fascias, which project 100mm (4in.) in front of the hanging rails – close enough to conceal the hooks and generous enough for easy removal and replacement. These rails also support shelves, concealed behind the fascias.

When not concealing and therefore sharing their profile with the rails, the fascias move freely in three dimensions, turning in to meet but finishing 25mm (1in.) from the face of walls, as if hovering, casting more complex shadows and coping with irregularities in the surface of existing walls.

Fascias on the lower floor have a hammered, patinated finish reminiscent of colours and textures in the painted ceiling on the floor above. Fascias at that level are white in deference to the ceiling, which is distanced from the new white floor and walls by a lowered perimeter zone that carries strips of recessed downlighters over the clothing and conceals the uplighters that illuminate the painted pattern on the ceiling.

RIGHT
The hanging rails, white on the upper floor and patinated on the lower, support hanging garments and accessory shelves. They sweep down to separate product sections and up to decorate the upper walls. The original ceiling painting is framed by the lowered perimeter element and washed by the lights concealed in it.

ELEVATION, SCALE 1:50

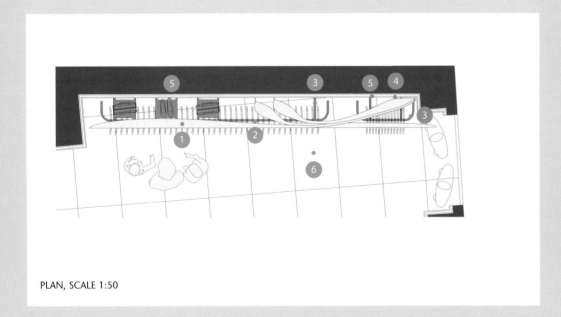

PLAN, SCALE 1:50

ABOVE
Plan and elevation of typical ground floor installation
1 Fascia piece – supported off hanging rail
2 Hanging rail – straight on plan, curved on elevation
3 Support rail with spigot fixing concealed behind wall lining
4 Plasterboard wall lining
5 Shelves supported on hanging rails
6 1200 x 600mm (42¼ x 23⅝in.) white composite floor tiles

OPPOSITE PAGE, TOP
Section
1 Fascia piece – supported off hanging rail
2 Wall-mounted mirror
3 New wall to conceal air conditioning and lighting
4 Shelf

OPPOSITE PAGE, BOTTOM LEFT
Ground floor plan
1 Entrance
2 Fascia/hanging rail
3 Mannequins
4 Display plinth

OPPOSITE PAGE, BOTTOM RIGHT
'Quilted' plinths

SECTION, SCALE 1:50

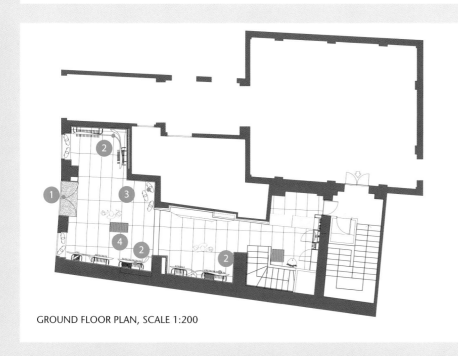

GROUND FLOOR PLAN, SCALE 1:200

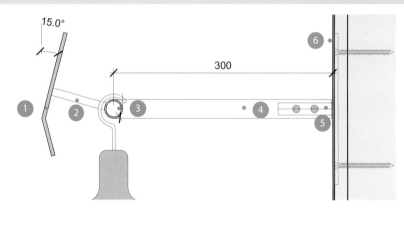

DETAIL, SECTION A2, SCALE 1:5

DETAIL, SECTION A4, SCALE 1:5

OPPOSITE PAGE, TOP LEFT

On the ground floor the colour of the patinated, hammered finish relates to the new floor pattern and anticipates the existing painted ceiling on the upper level.

OPPOSITE PAGE, BOTTOM LEFT

The thin sheet is hammered for texture.

OPPOSITE PAGE, BOTTOM RIGHT

Sections through fixture A
1 Fascia
2 10mm (⅜in.) steel tube
3 20mm (¾in.) steel hanging rail
4 20mm (¾in.) steel tube (slides over spigot arm and tightened with screws)
5 Spigot fixed through wall lining to existing wall
6 Plasterboard and skim
7 Wall battens

RIGHT

Elevations of typical wall installation
Hanging rails are restricted to accessible heights
1 Fascia
2 Hanging rail
3 Shelf supported off rail

BELOW RIGHT

Plan of typical wall installation
1 Fascia
2 Hanging rail
3 Support arm fixed to wall
4 Shelf

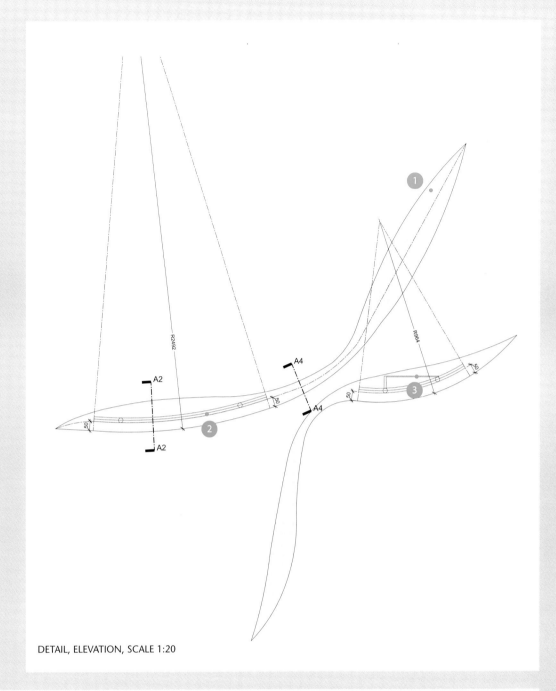

DETAIL, ELEVATION, SCALE 1:20

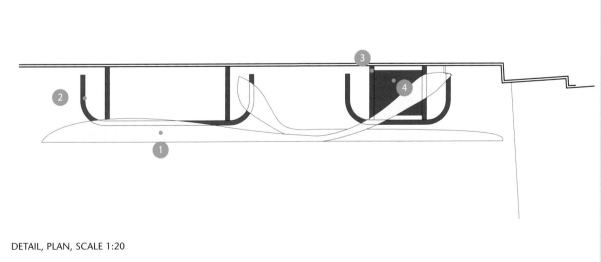

DETAIL, PLAN, SCALE 1:20

2.MOOD, TALLINN
VLS INTERIOR ARCHITECTURE

The designers were instructed to create an interior with a strong image and a distinctive identity that would set it apart from the other new clothes shops that were proliferating in Estonia. Its location in a recently developed area of Tallinn freed it from any obligation to respond to local architectural precedents.

The original building shell had little direct connection to the street, with floor-to-ceiling walls set back from the inside face of the windows to form a backdrop for window display. These walls have been retained but their internal faces are now treated as light boxes with fluorescent strip lights behind folded, translucent acrylic covers that are screwed back to the original wall surface. They make a backdrop for side-hung clothes displays.

Tubular clothes rails are suspended from the ceiling around the perimeter walls by woven metal wires and anchored at one end to the floor for stability. They also curve into the space between window and inner wall. Clothes hangers hook into slots cut into the back of the tubes. An adaptation of the hanging tube, resting on the floor at one end and bent back to form a base support at the other, provides free-standing floor display.

The illuminated ceiling area, which turns down the face of the wall behind the counter to create the dominant element of the interior, also uses the translucent acrylic sheet, supported on timber framing, and backlit by fluorescent strips. The impact of the light is increased by reflective foil on the wall and ceiling surfaces.

The counter and other pieces of floor-mounted display furniture are typified by what appear to be extreme cantilevered planes but are, in fact, supported along the midpoint of their long axis by sheets of frameless acrylic, which will be further concealed by any products displayed in front of them.

RIGHT
Backlit translucent acrylic sections are cut into the new ceiling and wall planes. Suspended and floor-mounted metal tubes act as hanging rails.

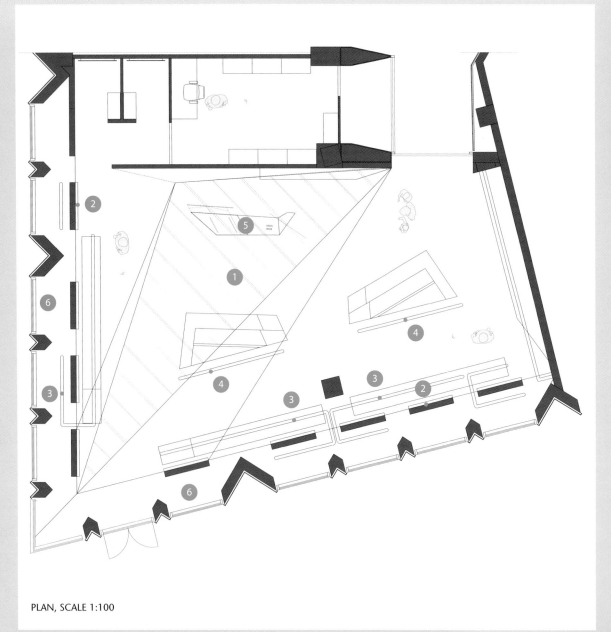

PLAN, SCALE 1:100

LEFT
Plan
1 Backlit ceiling area overhead
2 Internally illuminated wall boxes
3 Suspended hanging rails
4 Floor-mounted hanging rails
5 Counter position
6 Window display zone

BELOW LEFT
Sheets of clear acrylic fixed, without frames, between the solid elements of floor display units increase the apparent length of cantilevers.

BELOW RIGHT
MDF allows great precision in the making of components.

BELOW
Regular right-angled drawers and shelves are encased within the faceted outer shell of the counter.

BOTTOM LEFT
The heads of clothes hangers are hooked into slots cut into suspended painted steel tubes.

TOP & MIDDLE RIGHT
Letters and slots cut into a steel flat provide hanging rails in changing rooms. The folded end is screwed to the wall.

BOTTOM RIGHT
Folded acrylic lightboxes line the walls between sales floor and window display.

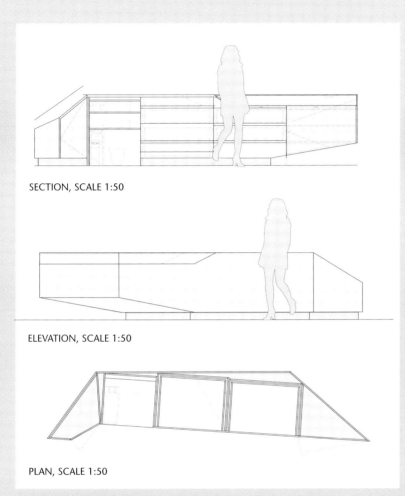

SECTION, SCALE 1:50

ELEVATION, SCALE 1:50

PLAN, SCALE 1:50

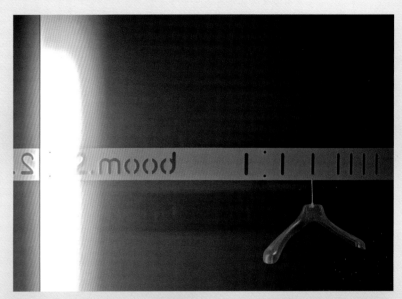

FOOD & HOUSEHOLD

SUZUKAKE HONTEN, FUKUOKA
CASE-REAL

Suzukake Honten is a chain of luxury pastry shops and tea rooms and this is its flagship store in the historic Japanese merchant city of Fukuoka. The design draws heavily on traditional form and ritual and includes a Saho, or tearoom, and a Kaho, or pastry shop.

The pastry shop is treated as an inner sanctum. Its core is a 9m (30ft)-long display counter, dramatically cantilevered at both ends. Behind it, set in a recess, is a stone-clad block that supports the rituals of service, while the potentially untidy elements necessary for wrapping and paying are concealed behind short walls of black textured plaster.

Single frameless sheets of glass make up the three sides and top of the display counter. Pastries are accessed by a series of hinged doors of reconstructed square-sectioned bamboo strips that match those that screen the long window wall opposite. The strips in this floor-to-ceiling screen are connected horizontally by black metal tubes that ensure even spacing and rigidity.

The Kaho has its own entrance and also shares a second with the Saho, although a short wall shields it from casual intrusion. The tea room is more welcoming – comparatively densely furnished with purpose-built but conventional furniture, and more visible and accessible from the street. It shares a bamboo screen (here against a windowless wall) and the black textured plaster walls with the Kaho but substitutes a moss green carpet, which runs up to and over the raised counter area, for the white soap-finished oak floorboards.

ABOVE RIGHT
Detail of the reconstructed bamboo screen, spaced and braced by metal tube.

RIGHT
Plan
1 Kaho – pastry shop
2 Bamboo screen
3 Saho – tea room
4 Cantilevered display counter
5 Service counter
6 Wrapping/paying
7 Counter
8 Kitchen

OPPOSITE PAGE
The 9m (30ft) cantilevered display counter provides drama. Its bamboo access doors reflect the floor-to-ceiling screen which fronts the long window wall. The service counter is set back in the recess.

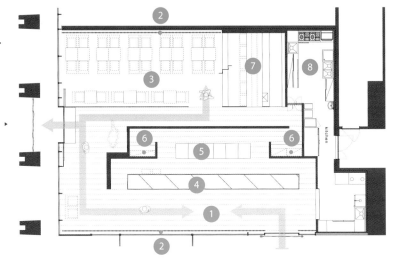

PLAN, SCALE 1:200

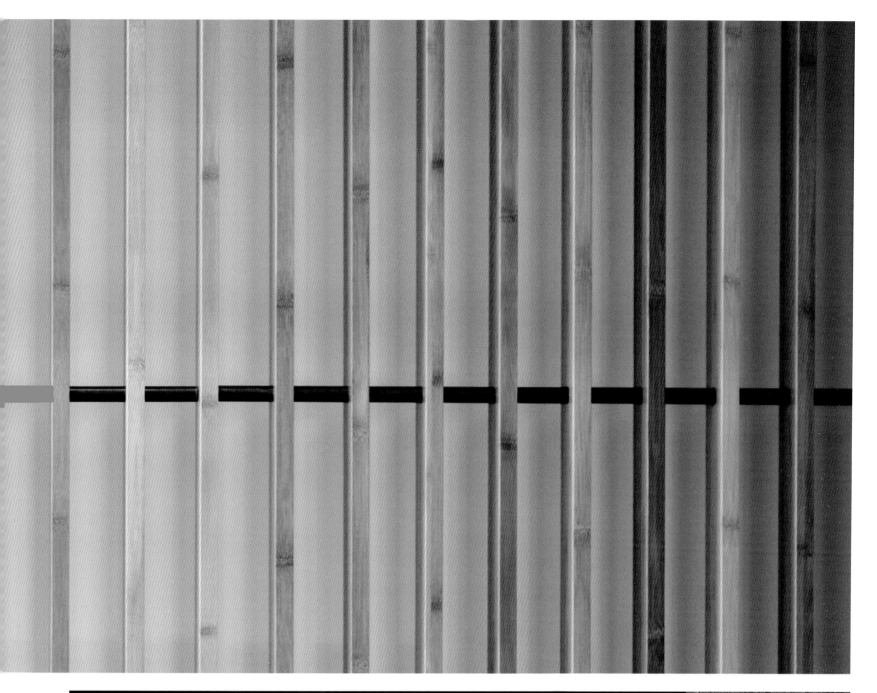

OPPOSITE PAGE, TOP
A second bamboo screen links the tea room to the pastry shop.

OPPOSITE PAGE, BOTTOM
The back of the display cabinet folds down for access. The top of each section is grooved to meet the glass top. The stone-clad service counter sits in the recess behind.

RIGHT
Oak floorboards with a white soap finish meet black polished plaster walls.

BELOW RIGHT
The tea room carpet flows onto the counter platform. The steps stop against a steel sheet on which the counter top rests.

UNAGI,
YANAGAWA
STAD

Unagi is the Japanese word for freshwater eels, a national delicacy, most often eaten during summer, with midsummer's day designated as the special day for their consumption. As with so many traditional Japanese activities, detailed rituals surround their preparation and consumption, and the associated reverence is clearly manifested in the quality of design and construction seen in this small eel shop and office. It is located within the shell of a utilitarian warehouse in the provincial city of Yanagawa, a popular destination for Japanese tourists because of its canals, and the eels they contain.

The project is characterized by the choice of burnt and charred cedar as the cladding material for exterior and interior walls. This is inspired by the traditional use of charcoal in the grilling of eels. The near-black wood is the project's defining colour and texture and is complemented by the smooth grey precision of the concrete walls and floor. The near-white wood of the Hans Wegner 'Wishbone' chairs and the rough stone step between levels, which has the tonal values of the concrete and the texture of the cedar, provide a visual bridge between both.

An existing change of level creates a platform, which has been devoted to the glass table for formal tasting of the products, and prompts the concrete upstand in the lower area that ensures that the height of the black walls remains constant throughout the different spaces. This precise thinking is evident in all detailing; in the frameless junctions between cedar boards and floor and ceiling, between glass and glass, glass and timber, glass and concrete. The quality of the details does not demand innovative techniques but is dependent on dedicated workmanship of the highest standard.

ABOVE
Chairs and a stone step make visual bridges between the black cedar and grey concrete.

ABOVE RIGHT
The charred cedar boards are the dominant and defining element within the interior, meeting the floor and walls directly, without skirting or cornice.

RIGHT
The refinement of the project sits incongruously in its industrial context.

FAR RIGHT
The office, while without the rich materiality of the other areas, displays the same precision of thinking and making.

HOUSE OF BLUE,
NEW YORK
STUDIO MAKKINK & BEY

Droog, the Dutch design collective, asked their collaborators, Makkink & Bey, to 'break the norms of store design' for their third shop, which sells small objects, limited-edition pieces and provides space for temporary exhibitions. They asked for an interior that would reflect their primary identity as a retailer of conceptual objects and in which all the component parts would be prototypes that might be customized to meet the particular demands and constraints of customers' own environments.

The objects for sale, the elements that display them and the original building structure are blended visually but the primary role of the new elements is to create contexts against which the Droog collection may be displayed and better understood.

The room at entrance level is dominated by representations of fragments of a house cut from blue polystyrene foam. These fragments act as shop fittings but may also be 'materialized' or translated into an appropriate 'real' medium such as wood or clay and fine-tuned for specific environments. The blue foam is a three-dimensional blueprint for possibilities.

The second installation, at basement level, performs as a wall that encloses the staircase and an office. The elements that project from the wall and the profiles cut into it may be translated into tables, benches and stools and are sold in flat-pack form. The production of all these pieces exploits CNC (computer numerical control) cutting techniques, and production information may be emailed to manufacturers throughout the world, initiating global distribution but local supply and production.

The principle may be applied as effectively to the creation and construction of all or parts of interiors and may be particularly appropriate in the territory of retail design, where global brands require global homogeneity.

RIGHT
The foam wall shelves and writing table, acting as display objects, may also be sold and translated into appropriate, durable materials.

OPPOSITE PAGE, TOP
At entrance level the existing building elements are left untouched while the blue foam house fragments provide contexts for the objects displayed.

OPPOSITE PAGE, BOTTOM
The numbered cut-outs on the right transform into the three-dimensional forms on the left and the objects on the floor, an explanation of the CNC process.

KVADRAT,
STOCKHOLM
RONAN & ERWAN BOUROULLEC

The brief required that the curtain and upholstery fabrics produced by Kvadrat should be wholly integrated into the design of their new showroom. The designers evolved a partitioning system of interlocking fabric-covered tiles.

Foam plastic core elements were covered in a selection of Kvadrat's coloured fabrics. Small 'lugs' on each tile were folded and inserted into slots in adjoining tiles to create semi-rigid curtains that provide substantial separation of functions within the showroom and bring a particular acoustic quality to the different spaces they define. The interlocking devices give a strong three-dimensional quality to the walls. A modified tile, without fixing lugs was developed for edge use. Construction is simple to understand and, once the hanging rails have been positioned, no expertise is required to assemble the 'walls'. The interlocking system makes reorganization of colours and openings simple.

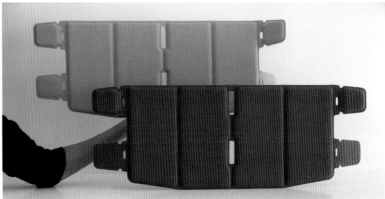

Door openings are self-supporting and make no loading demands on the tiled walls in which they are set. They may be simply repositioned in response to layout changes. They, and all other rigid display fittings and furniture, are manufactured from Douglas Fir, which provides a natural warmth that complements the tiles' textures and colours.

In their first assembly of the partitioning the designers hung tiles from point fixings but in later versions they developed a suspension rail system, with both straight and curved components, onto which the top row of tiles may be slid. This simplifies the assembly process and allows even distribution of the weight of the wall while also making the tiles hang more evenly.

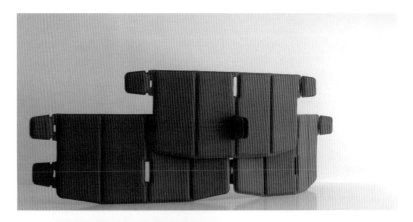

TOP RIGHT
Tiles provide subtle colour variation, three -dimensional texture and are adaptable to a variety of applications.

MIDDLE RIGHT
The basic tile.

RIGHT
The interlocking system.

BOTTOM RIGHT
Once interlocked the units have both structural stability and flexibility.

ABOVE

The use of Douglas Fir for floors, doors and bespoke display fittings and furniture provides a smooth warmth that complements the colour and texture of the tile walls. Gradation of colour accentuates the impact of natural light from tall windows.

RIGHT

Lighting dramatizes colours and textures. The door element sits with structural and visual independence within the wall. A foam plastic tile core lies on the table.

VILASOFA, ROTTERDAM
TJEP.

VilaSofa is a new furniture brand that produces medium-priced goods and guarantees to deliver all displayed models within 48 hours of purchase. The interior of the shop/showroom retains the volume and openness of a warehouse shell, appropriate to the idea of fast delivery, but within it are elements that suggest domestic environments, albeit on an inflated scale.

Customers enter beneath a mezzanine and pass product displays in a series of 'rooms' loosely defined by over-scaled geometric screens before reaching the double-height volume that contains the stair to the upper level with similar subdivisions and display areas.

The dominant element in the double-height space is a white painted plaster wall that separates the display floors from the service area at the rear. This double-height partition is indented with pictograms representing external and internal building elements: windows, a balcony, a chandelier. Some are void but where they need to be closed off to mask some utilitarian function, reveals are deepened and the recessed plane is painted in red stripes to maintain the two dimensional integrity of the white plane. Other two-dimensional vinyl graphics on walls and in the bespoke carpet are derived from transportation iconography.

Pieces of furniture, inspired by picnic benches, are dotted around the display floor to allow customers to discuss purchases between themselves and with staff. The cash desk, on wheels, can be brought to customers as they stand by, or sit on, their proposed purchase. These pieces, over-scaled like the screens, use familiar materials – pine wood, white laminates, painted metal – and are assembled using simple, clear construction techniques, suggesting company commitment to generosity of materials and quality of construction.

RIGHT
Large-scaled geometric screens subdivide the areas above and below the mezzanine.

ELEVATION, SCALE 1:100

ABOVE
Elevation of 'cut-out' wall

BELOW
Plans
1 Display areas
2 Double-height space
3 'Cut-out' wall
4 Service area
5 Void
6 Stair to mezzanine

GROUND FLOOR, SCALE 1:400

MEZZANINE PLAN, SCALE 1:400

ABOVE
The double-height space is dominated by the white wall with its graphic cut-outs.

ABOVE RIGHT
Heavy and simple shop furniture and geometric and simple graphics sit comfortably in the double-height volume.

RIGHT
The mobile cash desk brings the mechanics of ordering and paying to the customers sitting on their selected product.

FOOTWEAR

CAMPER, LONDON
TOKUJIN YOSHIOKA

It is always difficult, and probably foolish, to attempt to create allusions to natural forms within an interior. The normal materials and processes of construction are not suited to making the slight but inevitable variations that characterize every component of every natural form.

This interior, inspired by an earlier installation in which the designer used 30,000 sheets of tissue to represent a snowscape, suggests that it is possible to make a convincing suggestion of natural form, retaining its essential fragility and variability by avoiding too literal a reproduction of a natural precedent.

Fragments, approximately 200mm (8in.) square, of stretch fabric are loosely gathered to suggest floral shapes and are then sewn, approximately every 100mm (4in.), to the fabric covering wall panels and chairs. The frequent placement of individual 'florets' ensures that they are supported by those around them and that they retain their three-dimensionality. The inevitable minor undulations generated by the loose gathering of fabric add to the suggestion of organic form. The intense red of the long wall and its mirrored reflection refers to Camper's logo but the colour variations used for the chairs evoke those found in nature.

The shop unit is extremely narrow but its apparent width is increased by the mirror-lined wall that reflects the red 'foliage'. This tactic usually does little more than draw attention to a room's limitations but here the drama of the red wall provides something worth reflection. The lowered ceiling area, hard against the mirror, reads as one with its reflection and suggests a physical continuity that understates the mirror's presence.

All other elements in the shop – display surfaces, counter and lowered ceiling area – are strictly geometrical and painted white, providing the most extreme contrast to the organic fabric flowers. The plinth that stretches the length of the red wall conceals the light source that washes it and accentuates its organic unevenness.

ABOVE
The organic textures of 'floral' wall and chairs contrast with the planar geometry of other principal elements in the shop. The mirrored wall doubles the drama.

RIGHT
Soft fabric mimics the irregularities of natural forms.

OPPOSITE PAGE, TOP
Hard white display surfaces complement the fabric. The light source in the back of the low plinth washes the red wall, emphasizing its organic irregularity.

OPPOSITE PAGE, BOTTOM
Tonal variations in the chair fabric further suggest the variations found in nature

CAMPER, PARIS
RONAN & ERWAN BOUROULLEC

This Camper store, like the previous example, relies on textiles to transform a conventional shop unit into the assertive statement that characterizes the brand's other outlets. As with the designers' project for Kvadrat (page 166), the textiles are hung from the ceiling but here they suggest heavy quilted blankets rather than interlocking rigid tiles.

The strongly coloured, back-stitched blankets partially cover walls and provide slabs of strong, non-reflective colours against the brand's trademark red paint, which coats the existing walls of the double-fronted shop unit. The blankets are cut at angles and hung irregularly to break up the received boundaries of the shop. Some overlap, further eliminating right angles, verticals and horizontals. Others hang from the ceiling, away from walls, separating spaces for customers and spaces for staff. The thickly padded, quilted fabric also changes the acoustics of the space so that the visual and aural experience gently confounds the expectations that customers bring with them. The visual texture of the quilts changes as parallel lines of stitching are replaced by the squared configurations of upholstery buttons.

The furniture, painted red to match the walls, is from a collection created by the designers for domestic use and chosen to accentuate the simplicity of the installation. Shoes, as is standard procedure in Camper shops, are principally set out on tables. Some here rest on small pieces of blanket that provide a soft and coloured contrast to the tables' hard-edged reds. Others are supported on rods that project directly from the painted, plastered walls; these rods and the shadows they cast are as important as wall decoration as they are as a practical display system.

ABOVE
Quilted blankets hang loosely, overlapping and angled, remodelling the interior visually – and acoustically.

RIGHT
Rods project to support shoes and cast shadows. A length of quilt transforms the standard table.

MIDDLE
Upholstery buttons change the visual texture of the blankets.

FAR RIGHT
Green quilts define the staff zone. A fragment of quilt makes the table a bench.

KYMYKA, MAASTRICHT
MAURICE MENTJENS

This shop occupies the ground floors of two early twentieth-century residential buildings. The beam, which replaces the load-bearing wall that originally separated the units, is supported at its midpoint on a mirror-clad steel column. Two chimney breasts are retained and also clad in mirror to a height of 900mm (35⅜in.) above floor level, for the benefit of customers trying on shoes, and to suggest that remnants of the heavy original structure are floating above the floor. One half of the new space retains the original domestic-scaled windows, the other a low display window installed in the 1970s.

Some original plasterwork detail remains and its simple horizontal lines are echoed in the wall-mounted shelves that link the two areas. Walls, beams, ceilings and shelves are painted white to unify and simplify the potentially disjointed remnants of the original buildings and to complement the colour and complexity of the shoes. The visual unity is reinforced by the timber-clad cabinets that line the walls and which contain storage and services, with display boxes and customer seating cut simply and squarely into them. Only the sales counter projects into the room.

The dominant elements in the interior are the vertical stainless steel tubes, extruded to varying heights and fixed to a regular grid plan in the sprung floor. Some act as plinths on which shoes rest lightly, fixed by magnetic clamps, and are presented as floating abstractions, seeming to defy gravity. The magnetic pads, when apparent, cause a certain frisson as they suggest a bolt crudely piercing the sole of these objects of desire.

TOP RIGHT
Stainless steel tubular plinths are concentrated in front of the principal window.

RIGHT
Shoes sit lightly, and apparently precariously, on top of selected plinths.

OPPOSITE PAGE
Mirrored surfaces break up the solidity of columns and walls. Continuous lengths of cantilevered shelves unify wall planes running across the original windows.

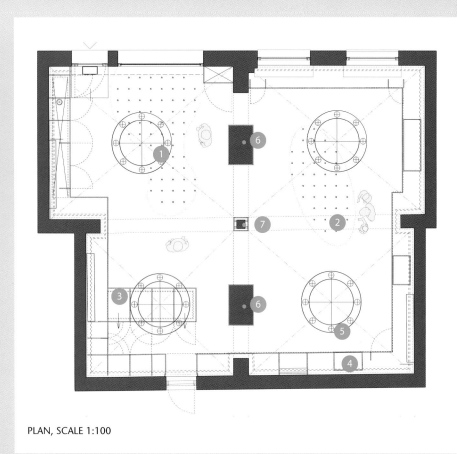

PLAN, SCALE 1:100

LEFT
Plan
1 Tubular plinths cluster in front of the main display window, next to the entrance
2 Plinths cluster in the middle of the inner room
3 Storage units cling to the wall, except for the counter, which projects into the room in line with a chimney breast
4 Seats are set into the perimeter storage
5 Chandelier
6 Former chimney breast
7 Mirrored column

BELOW
Section
1 Seating within storage unit
2 Mirror on original chimney breast
3 Mirrored casing on new column
4 Storage cabinets also conceal services
5 Shelves pass in front of original windows

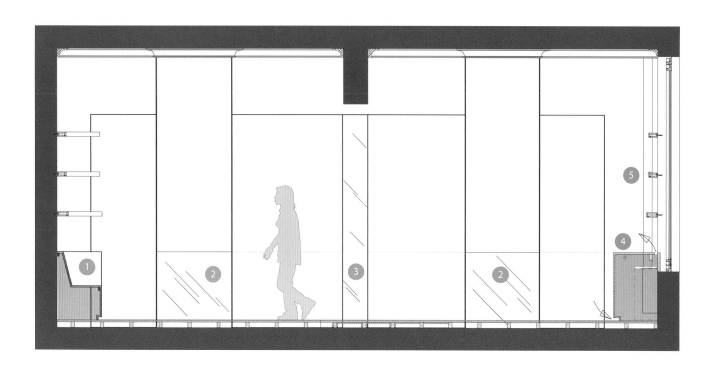

SECTION, SCALE 1:50

RIGHT

1 Steel insert
2 50mm (2in.)-diameter stainless steel tube
3 Threaded inner steel rod screwed into upper and lower tubes
4 Finished floorboards
5 Composite board subfloor
6 Composite board to increase depth and stability of tube
7 Timber batten nailed to bearer
8 Timber bearer to align

BELOW

The plinths rise from the floor with no apparent anchoring devices. Magnetized discs lock, through the sole of the shoe, on the steel insert at the top of each tube and are strong enough to hold shoes in position horizontally.

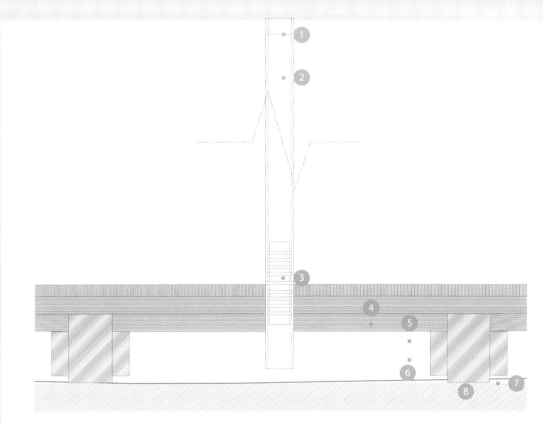

DETAIL, SCALE 1:5

THE SHOE BOX:
PEDDER RED FLAGSHIP STORE, HONG KONG
NHDRO

The need for an accessible display of extensive product ranges makes it difficult to give flagship shoe shops the single significant gesture that encapsulates their brand identity. This project uses the storage area, a utilitarian necessity to accommodate a full range of sizes, as the pretext for the two storey tower that dominates the more familiar areas allotted to selection and fitting – and builds on the pun in the shop's name.

The new tower/box is clad in plywood panels in which the grains of the stained oak veneers are laid in a pattern that suggests the hand stitching of well-made shoes. The display recesses are located within the modules of the stitching pattern and reveal the oak panels to be no more than the thin outer skin to a vibrant red interior, a second visual pun that refers to the brand name. The recesses have no back panels so that customers are given glimpses of the coloured core.

While the more public world of the shop – that inhabited primarily by customers – employs a conventional vocabulary of veneered wall panels and floor boards, occasionally counterpointed by concrete, all elements within the tower are painted uniformly red so that, while customers are unlikely to enter this service area, they catch glimpses that will leave no doubt about the nature of its interior.

The higher light levels within the tower create an environment that is significantly different from that in the perimeter public zones where the detailing of frameless doors and sharp edges is restrained and precise. The language of the inner tower is precise but less refined, determined by utilitarian metal elements, standard fixings that are clearly visible and typified by components of the spiral stair.

TOP RIGHT
The two-storey storage tower, with its 'woven' veneer and glimpses of its red core, dominates the street frontage.

RIGHT
Detailing of public areas is restrained, more subservient to the product display.

OPPOSITE PAGE, TOP LEFT
The tower slips through a void at upper floor level. The red slots sit within the matrix of the veneered strips and their intense colour complements the tones and textures of the veneers.

OPPOSITE PAGE, TOP RIGHT
In the tower, detailing remains precise, with individual elements defined by shadow gaps, so that the glimpses given to customers consolidate the impression of quality.

OPPOSITE PAGE, BOTTOM
The interior of the tower has a wholly different brash and utilitarian aesthetic.

SHOEBOX,
NEW YORK
SERGIO MANNINO STUDIO

Expensive shoes and accessories are admired for qualities that are aesthetic rather than practical. They may be exhibited reverently, as objets d'art, or their essentially decorative and hedonistic role can be acknowledged, celebrated, and enjoyed.

The Shoebox designers chose the second approach, risking a visually complex solution that might have overwhelmed the products. They relied on an extensive palette of colour and pattern for impact, which can be a dangerous strategy because people appear to have few inhibitions about expressing an opinion on colour, perhaps assuming that applying paint needs no specialist knowledge and that everyone's opinion is a valid one.

In Shoebox, 200 MDF panels, which sit slightly proud of the supporting walls, are finished predominantly with gloss lacquers and, occasionally, with patterned fabrics and linoleums that provide focal points in the expanse of colour. The panels have three sectional profiles. Vertical panels are used purely as vehicles for colour, while those at 45 degrees and right angles to the vertical provide individual shelves for individual products. The system allows flexibility in display and decorative combinations.

While the light, fresh and very pretty colours – closer to those more normally found in fashion than in interior design – are the dominant ingredient in the composition, they are supported by a battery of other less assertive devices. The lacquered stepped structure in the shop window is mirrored in the cashier's desk at the rear and the two are connected by lacquered elements for seating and display. The desk sits in front of the folds of a velvet curtain, which matches the green of the walls, and softens what are otherwise hard and glossy finishes. This solution is now used for Shoebox shops throughout the world.

ABOVE
The interior is dominated by the collage of lacquered panels and shelves. The stepped structure behind the window is mirrored by the cash desk at the back. The two are connected by plinths that serve for seating and display.

RIGHT
Lacquered central plinths act as display units. L-shaped panels turned on their side support the glass shelves. Cushions mark seating positions.

FAR RIGHT
Flat panels provide colour and occasional patterns. L-shaped panels act as shelves.

LEFT
Most shelves are white. Some are coloured to complement the product displayed on them.

BELOW
Elevation
1 Window display
2 Upholstered fabric
3 Linoleum finish
4 Mirror

Plan
1 Street
2 Belt display
3 Panels/shelves
4 Central plinth
5 Counter

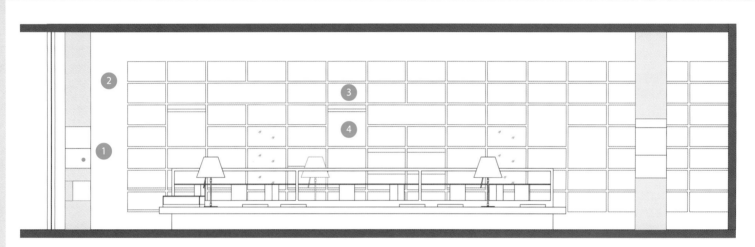

ELEVATION, SCALE 1:50

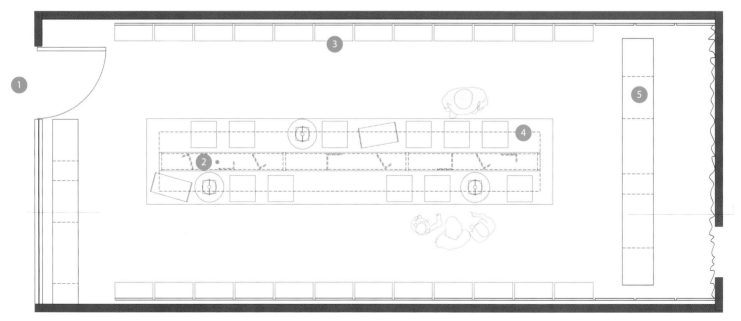

PLAN, SCALE 1:50

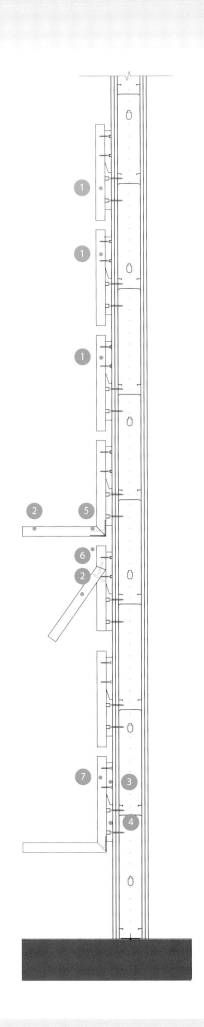

LEFT
Section through display wall
1 Removable panel
2 Removable shelf
3 French key, anchored on shelf
4 French key, anchored on studs
5 Wood dowel
6 Steel angle
7 Display shelves, lacquered MDF

ABOVE
Mirrors respect the grid and have the same dimensions and fixing methods as the lacquered panels.

RESOURCES

ARGENTINA

Dieguez Fridman Arquitectos & Asociados
Alvarez Thomas 198
1427 Buenos Aires
Argentina
T +54 11 45 51 99 00
www.dieguezfridman.com.ar
Ayres

CHINA

nhdro (Neri & Hu Design and Research Office)
88 Yuqing Road, Shanghai
China 200030
T +86 21 6082 3777
F +86 21 6082 3778
info@nhdro.com
www.nhdro.com
The Shoe Box

SAKO Architects
1801 and 1803, Tower 8
JianWaiSOHO, No. 39
East 3rd Ring Road
Chaoyang District
Beijing 100022
CHINA
T +86 10 5869 0901
F +86 10 5869 1317
www.sako.co.jp
Romanticism 2

ESTONIA

VL Sisearchitektuur Oü
Gonsiori 5A-13
Tallinn 10117
Estonia
T +3726600111
info@vis.es
2. Mood

FRANCE

Mathieu Lehanneur
Duende Studio, 8 Cite Veron
75018 Paris
France
T +33 6 42 23 64 33
press@duendestudio.fr
Laboshop

Ronan et Erwan Bouroullec
23, rue du Buisson Saint Louis
75010 Paris
France
T +33 1 42 00 40 33
www.bouroullec.com
Camper Paris, Kvadrat

GERMANY

eins:33 GmbH
Architecture and Interior Design
Dreimühlenstrasse 19
80469 Munchen
Germany
T +49 89.461 33 65 ext 0
F +49 89 461 33 65 ext 29
info@einszu33.de
Dressler Papeterie

Graft: Gesellschaft von Architekten mbH
Heidestrasse 50
10557 Berlin
Germany
T +49 30 306 45 103 ext 0
F +49 30 306 45 103 ext 34
berlin@graftlab.com
Opticon

Gonzales Haase
Pierre Jorge Gonzalez/Judith Haase/Atelier Architecture & Scenography
Strausberger Platz 19 D
10243 Berlin
Germany
T +49 30 25 296 181
F +49 30 25 296 182
www.gonzalezhaase.com
aas@gonzalezhaase.com
Antonios Markos Boutique

GREECE

Point Supreme Architects
Principals: Konstantinos Pantazis and Marianna Rentzou
Athens
Greece
info@pointsupreme.com
www.pointsupreme.com
Aktipis

ICELAND

Sruli Recht
Hólmaslóð 4
Reykjavík 101,
Fishpacking District
Iceland
T +354 5344238
www.srulirecht.com
Vopnabúríð

ITALY

Studio Fuksas
Piazza del Monte di Pietà
30 I-00186 Roma
Italy
T +39 06 68807871
F +39 06 68807872
office@fuksas.com
Armani

Studiometrico
Via Fontanesi 4
20146 Milan
Italy
T +39 02 45498389
mail@studiometrico.com
Bastard

JAPAN

Case-Real
1-9-8 Imagawa Chuoh-ku
Fukuoka 810-0054
Japan
T +81 92 718 0770
F +81 92 718 0777
futatsumata@casereal.com
Double OO, Note, Suzukake Honton

GENETO +pivoto
437-B Shimokuromon-cho
Nakagyo,
Kyoto 604 8355
Japan
T +81 75 203 2970
F +81 75 200 9787
info@geneto.net
Power Plant

Klein Dytham Architecture
AD Bldg 2F
1-15-7 Hiroo
Shibuya-ku
Tokyo 150-0012
Japan
kda@klein-dytham.com

Vertu
Sinato Inc., Chikara Ohno
Japan
T +81 3 6413 9081
F +81 3 6413 9082
central@sinato.jp
www.sinato.jp
Duras, Rolls

STAD, Toru Shimokawa
441-5 Oishimachi
Kurume-city
Fukuoka 830-0049
Japan
T & F +81 942 35 9858
stad@65x45.com
Unagi

Tokujin Yoshioka inc.
9-1 Daikanyamacho, Shibuya
Tokyo 150-0034
Japan
T +81 3 5428 0830
F +81 3 5428 0835
www.tokujin.com
Camper London, Pleats Please, Swarovski

THE NETHERLANDS

KUUB
sint nicolaasstraat 26 1
012 NK Amsterdam
The Netherlands
T +31 61 921 0915
info@kuub.nu
Precinct 5

Maurice Mentjens Design
Martinusstraat 20
6123 BS, Holtum
The Netherlands
T +31 46 481 1405
F +31 46 481 14 06
info@mauricementjens.com
Kymyka, Labels

Studio Makkink & Bey BV
P.O. Box 909
3000 AX Rotterdam
The Netherlands
T +31 10 425 8792
F +31 10 425 9437
www.studiomakkinkbey.nl
House of Blue

Tjep.
Veembroederhof 204
1019 HC Amsterdam
The Netherlands
T +31 20 362 42 96
F +31 20 362 42 99
www.tjep.com
Vilasofa

UXUS
Keizersgracht 174
1016 DW Amsterdam
The Netherlands
T +31 20 623 3114
F +31 20 421 7669
www.uxusdesign.com
Oilily

SPAIN

DearDesign
Tordera 66 local
Barcelona 08012
Spain
T +34 934 590 524
F +34 934 592 528
www.deardesign.net
Lurdes Bergada

SWEDEN

Guise
Katarina Vastra Kyrkgata 8
11625 Stockholm
Sweden
T +46 707 464235
www.guise.se
Fifth Avenue Shoe Repair

UK

apa
25 Lexington Street
London W1F 9AH
England
T +44 20 7439 4290
F +44 20 7439 4291
info@apalondon.com
www.apalondon.co.uk
Stella McCartney

Brinkworth
6 Ellsworth Street
London E2 0AA
England
T +44 20 7613 5341
F +44 20 7739 8425
www.brinkworth.co.uk
All Saints, Bastyan, Boxfresh

Caulder Moore
The Coach House
273a Sandycombe Road, Kew
London TW9 3LU
England
T +44 20 8332 0393
www.cauldermoore.co.uk
Ormonde Jayne

Eva Jiricna Architects
Third floor, 38 Warren Street
London W1T 6AE
England
T +44 020 7554 2400
F +44 020 7388 8022
mail@ejal.com
Boodles

Universal Design Studio Ltd.
35-42 Charlotte Road
London EC2A 3PG
England
T +44 207 033 3881
F +44 207 033 3882
www.universaldesignstudio.com
H+M Harjuku, H+M LA, Lotte

USA

Leong Leong
Principals: Christopher Leong
& Dominic Leong
157 Bowery
New York, NY 10002
USA
T +1 917 262 0027
F +1 917 677 8520
info@leong-leong.com
www.leong-leong.com
3.1 Philip Lim

Sergio Mannino Studio
45 Main Street, Suite 546
Brooklyn
New York, NY 11201
USA
T +1 718 855 5018
F +1 718 679 9688
info@sergiomannino.com
www.sergiomannino.com
Shoebox

CREDITS

All architectural drawings are supplied courtesy of the architects. In all cases every effort has been made to credit the copyright holders, but should there be any omissions or errors the publisher will be pleased to insert the appropriate acknowledgment in any subsequent editions of the book.

Aktipis Project team: Konstantinos Pantazis, Marianna Rentzou, Giorgos Pantazis; Photography: Yannis Drakoulidis

All Saints Design: Brinkworth with All Saints in-house design team; Photography: Louise Melchior

Antonios Marcos All images courtesy Gonzalez Haase/AAS; Copyright drawings: Gonzalez Haase/AAS; Copyright photographs: Thomas Meyer/Ostkreuz

Armani Design: Massimiliano Fuksas, Dorianna Fuksas; Photography: Ramon Prat (57) Studio Fuksas (59)

Ayres Design: principals Tristán Dieguez, Axel Fridman; Collaborators: Leonardo Buffa, Maria Carranza, Rosario Guiraldes, Belén Gándara; Structural Engineer: Sebastián Berdichevsky; Lighting consultant: Pablo Pizarro; Landscape design: Cora Burgin; Object design: MartinWolfson; Photography: Juan Hitters

Bastard Design: Lorenzon Bini and Francesco Murialdo with Marco Lampugnani; Structural consultant: Marco Clozza at Atelier LC; Photography; Guiliano Berarducci

Bastyan Photography: Louise Melchior

Boodles EJAL: Eva Jiricna, Duncan Webster, Jane Cameron, Vendula Zimandlova; Stairs: Clifford Chapman Metalworks Limited; Specialist Glass: Techniques Transparentes, Paris/ Hourglass, UK; Contractor: SD Shopfitting & Contracts Ltd.; Photography: Richard Bryant (14 top, 15) Katsuhisa Kida (14 bottom, 17, 19)

Boxfresh Photography: Louise Melchior

Camper London Photography: Koji Fujii/ Nácasa & Partners Inc. (top 174, top 175); Alessandro Paderni (bottom 174, bottom 175)

Camper Paris Photographs © studio Bourollec

Dressler Project team: Georg Thiersch, Florian Dressler, Eva Bruniecki Photography: Johannes Severlein

Double OO Design: Koichi Futatsumata; Builder: Ob; Photography: Hiroshi Mizusaki

Duras Photography: Takumi Ota
Precinct 5 Photography: Marcel van der Burgh

Fifth Avenue Shoe Repair Design: Jani Kristoffersen, Andreas Ferm; Builder: Guise AB; Furniture production: Guise AB; Photography: Jesper Lindstrom, Mattias Lindback (dressing room and white stair)

H+M Harajuku Photography: Takumi Ota

H+M LA Photography: John Edward Linden

House of Blue Photography: Ian Tong

Kvadrat Photographs p166 (top) and p167 © Paul Tahon, Ronan & Erwan Bouroullec; p166 (bottom 3 images) © studio Bouroullec

Kymyka Design: Maurice Mentjens, Johan Gielissen, Annet Butink, Paul Bovens; Photography: Leon Abraas

Labels Design: Maurice Mentjens, Johan Gielissen, Annet Butink, Paul Bovens; Interior: Schreurs Interieur Timmerbedrijf; Graphics: Groenergras; Photography: Arjen Schmitz

Laboshop Photography © Fabien Thouvenin

Lotte Photography courtesy of Lotte

Lurdes Bergada Design: Ignasi Llaurado, Eric Dufourd, Dorien Peeters; Photography: Pol Cucala

Note Design: Koichi Futatsumata; Builder: Kubota Real Estate Construction; Photography: Hiroshi Mizusaki

Oilily Photography courtesy of the architect

Opticon Design: Sven Fuchs, Gunhild Niggemeier, Julian Busch, Christoph Jantos, Alejandra Lillo; Carpenter: Thomas Kathrein, Kathrein Tischlerei und Innenausbau GmbH; Floor Covering Artwork: Tomas Kerwitz, Kult Carpet, Kerwitz & Kerwitz GbR; Upholstery: Nowel J. Polsterei und Galerie; Metal work: Stefan Fittkau, fittkau metallbau + kunstschmiede GmbH; Illuminated Advertising: André Koslitz, KOSLITZ WERBUNG; Floor Covering: Poodle 1400, 1467 Bianco und 1463 Vino Rosso, Objectcarpet; Upholstery/Fabric: Sky 1590, Kvadrat GmbH; Photography: Christian Barz

Ormonde Jayne Photography courtesy of the architect

Philip Lim Design: Chris Leong, Dominic Leong, Christa Mohn, Cody Zalk, Scott Rominger; Local Architect: Dadam S.D; Photography: Iwan Baan

Pleats Please Photography courtesy of the architect

Power Plant Design: Koji Yamanaka, Yuji Yamanaka, Asako Yamashita; Builder: Keji Tsujii, Eichiro Shiro; Engineer: Takashi Takamizawa; Curator: Masaaki Takahashi; Photography: Masano Kawano (Nacasa & Partners Inc)

Rolls Photography: Toshiyuki Yano
Romanticism Photography: Koji Fujii/ Nácasa & Partners Inc.

Stella McCartney Concept Architects: APALtd; Execution Architect (Milan): J+R Studio; Bespoke sculptural wall pieces designed by APA; Bespoke furniture designed by APA Ground floor coloured timber floor installation by Shay Alkalay and Yael Mer (Established & Sons); Photography: Nick Hufton

Swarovski Photography: Nácasa & Partners Inc.

Shoebox NY Design: Sergio Mannino, Francesco Scalettaris, Francesco Bruni Lighting design: Bill Pierro Jr. BP2 Photography: Sergio Mannino Studio The Shoe Box Design: Lyndon Neri, Rossana Hu; Photography: Derryck Menere

Suzukake Honten Design: Koichi Futatsumata; Builder: Ob; Photography: Hiroshi Mizusaki

2 Mood Photography with merchandise: Martin Siplane; without merchandise: Ville Lausmäe

Unagi Design: Toru Shimokawa; Photography: Kozi Hayakawa

Vertu Design: Astrid Klein, Mark Dytham, Miki Hisaeda, Shin Takahashi; Lighting: FDS (Tohru Gotoh, Takehide Yamane); Construction: D. Brain Co. Ltd (Masaru Mogaki, Etsuo, Keiichi Hirakawa, Katsuyoshi)

Vilasofa Design: Frank Tjepkema, Janneke Hooysmans, Leonie Janssen, Tina Stieger, Bertrand Gravier, Camille Cortet; Construction: Kloosterboer

Vopnabúríð Photographs by Marino Thorlacius

ABOUT THE CD

The attached CD can be read on both Windows and Macintosh computers. All the material on the CD is copyright protected and is for private use only.

The CD includes files for all of the drawings included in the book. The drawings for each building are contained in a folder labelled with the project name. They are supplied in two versions: the files with the suffix '.eps' are 'vector' Illustrator EPS files but can be opened using other graphics programs such as Photoshop; all the files with the suffix '.dwg' are generic CAD format files and can be opened in a variety of CAD programs.

Each image file is numbered according to its original location within the book and within a project, reading from left to right and top to bottom of the page, followed by the scale. Hence, '01_01_200. eps' would be the eps version of the first drawing of the first project in the book and has a scale of 1:200.

The generic '.dwg' file format does not support 'solid fill' utilized by many architectural CAD programs. All the information is embedded within the file and can be reinstated within supporting CAD programs. Select the polygon required and change the 'Attributes' to 'Solid', and the colour information should be automatically retrieved. To reinstate the 'Walls'; select all objects within the 'Walls' layer/class and amend their 'Attributes' to 'Solid'.